# CHAOS LOVES YOU

## So Let's Love It Back

### JOTHI DUGAR

The Chaos Guru

**BALBOA.**PRESS
A DIVISION OF HAY HOUSE

Balboa Press books may be ordered through booksellers or by contacting:

Balboa Press
A Division of Hay House
1663 Liberty Drive
Bloomington, IN 47403
www.balboapress.com
844-682-1282

Because of the dynamic nature of the Internet, any web addresses or links contained in this book may have changed since publication and may no longer be valid. The views expressed in this work are solely those of the author and do not necessarily reflect the views of the publisher, and the publisher hereby disclaims any responsibility for them.

The author of this book does not dispense medical advice or prescribe the use of any technique as a form of treatment for physical, emotional, or medical problems without the advice of a physician, either directly or indirectly. The intent of the author is only to offer information of a general nature to help you in your quest for emotional and spiritual well-being. In the event you use any of the information in this book for yourself, which is your constitutional right, the author and the publisher assume no responsibility for your actions.

Any people depicted in stock imagery provided by Getty Images are models, and such images are being used for illustrative purposes only. Certain stock imagery © Getty Images.

Print information available on the last page.

ISBN: 978-1-9822-6220-4 (sc)
ISBN: 978-1-9822-6222-8 (hc)
ISBN: 978-1-9822-6221-1 (e)

Library of Congress Control Number: 2021901253

Balboa Press rev. date: 01/22/2021

# Contents

## Dedication

This book is dedicated to my three amazing children, Shayana, Shaylan, and Jiyana for enabling me to transform myself, so that I can help millions of people in the world transform their lives.

Without my support system of my family and friends encouraging me, standing behind me, and challenging me, I could not be who I am today, and I wish more than anything in the world for every one of you out there to truly live your life to the fullest, and ride those waves of chaos freely, openly, and confidently.

## Introduction

Whether you are feeling distressed or overwhelmed, you have come to the right place. Our lives and jobs are filled with such high stress, demands, and well...chaos. I want you to know that you are not alone. That may not feel comforting at the moment, but I hope it at least helps you feel a sense of normalcy. You don't have to have to go through life suffering and working so hard just to find peace. In fact, peace is the minimum state we are going to aim for in this book.

What if I tell you that you are going to actually *thrive* in the chaos by the end of this journey? In fact, you might even want to invite the chaos in! Sound crazy? Well, have a little faith and just give this process a chance. I'm here to share with you the same methods that has helped me time and time again to create lasting change in my life, through life threatening health conditions, through trauma, through relationship challenges, and much more.

Chaos isn't going anywhere. Chaos loves you, so why not learn to love it back!

## Wait! Proceed with Caution

If you found this book, or if this book has somehow found you, let's cut to the chase. It is for a reason. It is no accident.

It is probably because there is something in your life, or perhaps many things, that are driving you to change. Maybe you've been searching for answers for years. Maybe you're healing from a pain you have experienced. I get it. I've been there myself.

Trust me on this—until you've actually found a way to process that pain and release the suffering from within, it is going to continue to follow you around getting nastier, harrier, and scarier.

The good news is that you have finally found this book. This is no coincidence.

Relax.

Take a deep breath.

You're in the right place, and I've got your back. We're going to go on this transformational journey together.

Where are you right now in your life?

Do you feel like you're living your wildest dreams?

Do you wake up excited every day?

Maybe you have a good life but you want *more* than just good.

Or maybe you are going through hell and feel no one understands you.

Maybe you're in a place of pain right now, feeling really down and overwhelmed.

Do you sometimes wish you could just snap your fingers and go back to a time in your life when you felt safe, protected, and had someone who loved you unconditionally? Do you feel that sometimes the people who you want to have your back are the ones you feel the most hurt by?

I hear you. Loud and clear.

Sometimes the people in your life who you really want to trust and have your back, are actually the ones hurting you the most.

Let's add to that. What if you can't count on the people you want to count on at your home or social setting, but you also have to be a leader in your workplace?

Who exactly are you bringing to the workplace? Is it your authentic self or does a different "version" of you go to the workplace?

Think about the people you work with. Can you really count on anyone there?

Who in your world do you actually trust to have your back… unconditionally?

It is ok if your answer is "I really don't know", because by the end of this journey, you will realize that your external world is a mirror of your internal world – and that means who you trust starts with trusting your inner authentic self. And guess what? That is ok my friend. Trust me when I say, you are NEVER really "alone."

So, tell me this. What have you tried so far to overcome your challenges? I'm going to take a wild guess and say that nothing you've tried so far has worked completely—otherwise you wouldn't be here right now reading this unusual beginning to your new journey. Right?

If you feel that you've had enough, and you're committed and ready to break through all the chaos in your life, you are in the right place.

Well, we're going to go deep, my friends. That is the only way real change happens. I wanted to write this book because I was sick and tired of all the superficial nonsense out there. I've seen it all. I've done it myself. And I know you don't need any more wishy-washy tactics that seem promising at first but only to produce temporary results. Enough is enough. Right?

I'm not going to lie to you and promise that this is going to be easy. Trust me—you don't want another light-and-fluffy guide or online course or some free PDF to get your life back. And I know you don't *need* that.

If you're tired of all the fake crap out there, all the empty promises, all the general stuff, and you're ready to give it all up and invest in yourself, say, "I am ready!"

Scream it from the top of your lungs and feel the strength of it.

## WARNING!

It will get uncomfortable. You may be asked to do things you've never done before. You may be asked to push aside distractions and really listen to your body, your mind, and your energy in ways you've suppressed before. You will have to face things that you have been avoiding or ignoring for far too long.

Now is the time to look those things in the eye.

You *are* ready for it. I have faith in you, and I'm all in by your side.

Trust me when I say that I am all in.

I got your back. We're all in this together.

# MY EPIPHANY MOMENT

Imagine being at the height of your career, feeling as if you have everything going for you. That was me. I thought, *I've finally made it.* I felt a great sense of pride and accomplishment having finally been recognized as a thought leader in my field. I had two wonderful kids and a third baby on the way. I was a textbook supermom. I felt like I had everything in life under control. And on the outside, it probably seemed like I did have everything under control.

It was supposed to be a moment of joy, laughter, and love—maybe even the best moment of my life—giving birth to my much-anticipated third baby.

But everything came crashing down when I found out I had six weeks to live if I didn't make some sudden decisions. Yup, you heard me. That's it, six weeks.

Control was stripped from my grasp. It was as if everything I worked so hard for was suddenly going to be taken away. I felt so confused and lost. I didn't know who to count on or where to turn. I kept showing up the best way I could, trying to save the world by being there for my husband, my kids, my work team, and my family. But no one was showing up for me in the way I needed them to.

The chaos around me and within me forced me to take a seat. I would have taken a knee if my body wasn't in excruciating pain from the neck down. I sat there, numb, knowing I had to be there for the world but wondering who was going to be there for me.

I had always been known for being determined and had loads of self-will. I had conquered everything in my path with perseverance and grace. I never took no for an answer, and I knew when I put my mind on something, I will achieve it. But I also knew that this time I needed something stronger than just my self-will. I needed a higher power, someone or something out there that will help guide me and carry me through.

I closed my eyes, took a deep breath, and asked the universe and any being higher than me, "What do I need to do about this?"

I felt desperate. I wanted to know why this freak "accident" happened to me. There had to be a logical and reasonable explanation right? I felt desperate to find cures other than the multiple surgeries the surgeons mandated that I needed, even though they didn't offer any clear end result. I felt that uncomfortable feeling of anxiety creeping in and I so eagerly wanted to get back to being my supermom/wife/leader of my world role. At least, that's what I thought I needed to do.

With all this chaos going on within me and around me, I could have given up and just went with the expectations of others. That would have been easier, right? I could have thought my life was ending and just believed the doctors. Or, I could have just put myself in the hands of the surgeons that mandated surgery but had no clue what they would accomplish.

I could have sat there, wallowing in disbelief and sadness, asking "why me?" to anyone who would listen. I could have tried to blame someone or something or surrendered to the chaos of my surroundings.

But I chose not to. I chose to believe that there was another way. There *had* to be another way, because…well….I was looking for it!

I looked at chaos straight in the eye and made a decision for myself to harness its power for good. My world needed me, but someone else needed me even more: myself.

That was me just four years ago. I promise I'll share pieces of my story with you throughout this journey. Things may seem scary and impossible at first, but I promise you that nothing is impossible. And I am with you every step of the way.

If you've come this far and haven't put the book down, congratulations!

You're ready to do the work.

You are all in!

Give yourself a pat on the back and shout it from the top of your lungs. Stop caring about who's watching.

You are investing in *yourself*. No one can do this for you. This is about you, for you, and by you. And guess what? You are worth it. Every single dollar, every single second, and every single breakthrough.

Let's do this together and release the weight of the chaos you've been holding on to all your life.

You, my friend, are ready.

Note: This is *not* a nice-to-read-on-the-train-while-I-commute-to-work type of book. This is a book you *do*—meaning get ready to take the actions that I walk you through in each chapter. Do the exercises that are meant to serve *you* and go all in on anything and everything you are called to do. This is how you will witness your own transformation. You told me you were done with just "information," so get yourself ready for some real *transformation*. Yes, that means you have to embody it, embrace it, and take action.

So, grab a pen, get yourself excited, and set your intention by saying the following: **I am ready to transform and invest in myself, and I will not stop until I attain the miracles that happen for me.**

*Chapter 1*

# THE OCEAN OF LIFE

*Your end goal in life is* **not** *to get to a state of calm and peace. – Jothi Dugar*

So, first off, I want to take a moment and say welcome my fellow chaos buster!

You made it this far, so let's get started and bust some chaos! Who knows, you may even bust some chaos myths that may have been affecting you.

Let's take a look at how you actually work. Please take a moment and put down your "I already know this" goggles. Trust me on this— knowing something and actually living it are two *very* different things.

I want you to think of your life like the ocean. Take a moment and get yourself in a relaxed position and visualize walking along the beach on a beautiful sunny morning. You see the sun glimmering on the ocean's surface. It is calm, pure, tranquil, and there are no waves in sight. You can feel the harmony and peace of this majestic creation of nature. The sun gently warms your face. The sand tickles the bottom of your feet. Everything feels peaceful and good and whole.

In fact, there is no denying that you may feel your energy restored just by thinking of the serenity of the ocean on a beautiful, sunny, early morning.

Ever since I was a little girl, I always marveled at the ocean. Just standing next to the water could refresh my soul. The good energy came in with the tide as the stress and discomfort washed out to sea. It was such a powerful feeling.

But let's go back to your visualization here. You're looking at the peaceful ocean and the water is still as glass. As you stare at the water with the sunlight shimmering on the surface, can you recall a time you felt this at peace in your mind, or body, or even in your energy?

It may feel restorative at the time, but what did you do when your chaotic energy returned? Let's face it, there is so much more to the ocean, and to your life, than a feeling of static serenity. How long do you think you can rest in that space before your heart grows bored and your mind craves stimulation?

This is *so* important. Getting to a state of calm is absolutely necessary. But, and this is a big but, there is a place and time for it.

**Your end goal in life is *not* to get to a state of calm and peace.**

Yup, I said it. Yes, there are gurus and healers and even scientists out there that preach that we must all get to a state of peace within ourselves. Yes, that is true, but only *if* we allow ourselves to wallow in a state of dismal chaos much of the time. How boring would your life be if it was as still as waveless water *forever*?

In fact, that is nearly impossible and unnecessary. Your mind was *designed* for chaos. You were born into chaos. The world was formed due to chaos. So, would you rather keep trying to get rid of it and go insane because it keeps following you around? Or do you want to *embrace* it and make the best use of it for your own good? Maybe even use that chaos for your own inner power?

Let's pause and talk about the different chaos wave types. Yes, there indeed are different *types* of chaos. If we revisit the ocean concept, we know the ocean is full of powerful forces. Have you ever seen a tsunami? You know, those massive natural disasters where something deep down below in the ocean acts as a trigger (think earthquake or sudden change in the ocean floor). The trigger causes the ocean to act abnormally. The ocean builds and builds and builds before crashing into and enveloping anything in its path. That, my friend, is Ugly Chaos.

Ugly chaos or should I say tsunami chaos is when a simple external trigger touches on a deep-rooted fear/insecurity/vulnerability in your subconscious mind and causes a disproportional reaction from you. It can also occur from a buildup of chaos in your life. And, guess what? You may feel that it never goes away.

If this is true, then you're constantly feeling like you have to deal with it. Maybe you try to distract yourself from this chaos, but it always rears its ugly head, growing bigger and stronger. I am sure you feel overwhelmed just thinking about it, right?

But wait, there is more. As you try to avoid, ignore, or look to others to solve your tsunami chaos for you, you might even be projecting your own inner chaos onto them without even realizing it.

Let's get a little deeper with our friend chaos here. Chaos follows you home. It comes into the office with you. It is right there as you get into an argument with your spouse. And it just keeps getting bigger and bigger.

Ahhh! Why can't it just go away?

Well, I'm sorry to say this, but chaos loves you. So until we learn to love it back, it isn't going anywhere. Let's take a look at how ugly chaos could be manifesting for you. It could be a feeling of low self-worth, or not knowing how to love yourself. Ugly chaos could be manifesting in your life simply because you're questioning the concept itself.

Do you feel yourself questioning your every move and wonder if you made the right decision? Are you allowing yourself to receive love from others in a way that makes you feel loved within? Do you feel scared of taking risks in your life unless you know there is a guaranteed outcome? I'm guessing you may even be your own worst critic, blaming yourself for things that were not even under your control.

Or, maybe you're a perfectionist trying to be the savior of the day for others. What's wrong with that, you ask? Well, are you trying to be perfect at everything you do because you're afraid of rejection? Or is it for validation from others? Are you trying to save the world and overachieve everything you touch trying to do it all, maybe to feel *seen?*

If you are trying to do any of the above and getting nowhere, then I'm sure you also have a ton of chaos running through you on a daily basis making you feel anxious, depressed, exhausted, apathetic, or all of the above. And, you're done, just done.

Just take a moment and take a deep, long breath. Let it out. Take another deep, long, breath, and let it out.

**There is a lighthouse nestled on the shore of this ocean of life.**

**Remember this: you are in the right place. You found this book.**

I know the ugly chaos can seem daunting and never-ending at first, but the good news is that it comes with an equally never-ending toolbox of strategies, modalities, and techniques that you can reach for anytime, anywhere. When you combine this toolbox with an immersive transformational program such as the one, I have created for you at www.jothidugar.com/services, you have the potential to enable remarkable changes within you to help release trauma, pain, chronic conditions, and anything else that is no longer serving you. These non-serving elements could be all the way from birth, childhood, or even for some - past lives.

One of the most notable ugly chaos triggers in my life would have to be my life-threatening health scare. I have three wonderful kids. All three were c-sections because the first one ended up being an emergency c-section and the other two were planned cesareans. I had the same doctor for the first two, and everything went well.

But when it was time for our third baby to enter the world, I was disappointed to find I'd have a different doctor who I did not know very well. I pushed my discomfort aside. The important goal was to deliver a healthy baby and I relied upon my trust in the hospital and management, people I thought I knew well, to help me achieve my goal.

My pregnancy was 100% normal. I thought I knew what to expect and I scheduled my c-section. My husband and I filled out the paperwork and when the time came, I was wheeled to the operating room. We delivered a beautiful healthy baby girl, just as we hoped, and I was taken to the recovery area.

Everything seemed to be okay for the most part, other than the part where my OB dashed out of the room as soon as the procedure was over, with no congratulations, or any explanation whatsoever. Well, that probably should have been my sign that my life, and ultimately our lives, were about to change.

When the on-call doctor came in to examine me, the color drained from his face after checking my incision. Immediately he called in a bunch of nurses and one by one, the color drained from their faces too. I laid there, trying to figure out what they were looking at. Did they see a ghost? Do I still have my legs?

I couldn't tell why their faces turned ghostly white, until the doctor started to explain that a typical c-section incision is between four to six inches long. This wasn't my first time. I knew that. But this time, I ended up with a *hip-to-hip incision*. That's twelve inches my friends.

They started asking me a bunch of questions as to how heavy or big the baby was. Normal position? Normal pregnancy? Yes, and yes. When none of my answers seemed to be the "easy reason," they gave up. "There must be a good explanation for this," they collectively agreed and let me rest. They told me to get in touch with the OB who performed my surgery.

Well, I would but she never came back to check on me! Ever.

I couldn't believe my ears. No one had an explanation for me.

I felt lost, confused, and angry. But I didn't have time for that. I needed to get myself strong enough to actually hold my baby and nurse, so I pushed through.

The moment they removed my IVs, the pain radiated throughout my body. I couldn't hold my newborn. I couldn't even move without passing out from excruciating pain. I stayed at the hospital four whole days, in immense pain, and no medication worked. And then I was sent home, told to rest, and assured everything would heal just fine, and was told stories of how much worse it could have been.

But I didn't heal on my own. In fact, I felt worse every day that went by. I couldn't move off my bed. I couldn't walk. I couldn't even hold myself, let alone the baby on my own. And, forget about actually being able to lie down to sleep. I sat in one reclined position day and night as that was the only position where I felt the pain as minimal as I possibly could.

I still had no answers, and this was really starting to get to me, my family, my friends, my team at work, and really everyone I knew.

The OB went missing in action for the next five months. The hospital management, the very people we thought we had a good relationship with based on previous experiences, failed us. They failed me. They had to protect their incompetent OB, so they covered up her negligence or should I say, downright incompetence.

To complicate the chaos within me even more, the excessive incision led to massive amounts of scar tissue build-up in my entire incision area. I was given no explanation as to why I was still in immense pain five months after giving birth and unable to move any part of my body without almost passing out. I felt helpless.

Here I was, a mother, wife, a global cyber, a dance director, a perfectionist, and a change agent in the world, expected to care for everyone who was depending on me - and I couldn't even get out of my own bed to care for myself.

I was hoping someone, anyone, could help me figure out why I was in excruciating pain. I could sit and I could lie down, but not comfortably. I needed answers. This was not the time for something so catastrophic to happen. I had to get back to work and lead my team. I wanted to be there for my kids. People needed me.

I barely managed to get myself out of the house to get a CT scan several months after the delivery. I thought that maybe the CT scan would reveal the answers I was looking for and all of this would come to an end.

Well, I thought wrong. I went from doctor to doctor, surgeon to surgeon, begging for answers. I saw five different surgeons, and not a single one could tell me why I was in so much pain.

"This looks very complicated. I'm not sure what we can do," they said. Or my favorite, "Let's book a surgery so I can go in and see what is going on. After that I'll have a better idea of the best course of action and we can schedule another surgery to actually fix it if I know how." It was so disheartening, and I continued to feel hopeless and exhausted.

The most competent surgeon out of the pack told me no one could figure out the extent of what was wrong with me since I was in pain from the neck down. But they were able to determine I had a freak type of double hernias. There was an actual separation of abdominal layers. The OB did not patch up all the layers of my abdominal muscles and my organs were in the wrong place because of it. In fact, they were not functioning properly. I was a medical freak show of the worst kind, or the 1% of time something rare like this happens, they said. Well lucky me! I made the cut to the 1%, just not in the way anyone would have ever wanted. And I was tired.

My body was weak. My organs were possibly shutting down. My core was decimated, and the doctors thought I was a good "case study" and seemed super excited to do multiple surgeries to boost their own curiosity and ego.

I felt scared, angry, sad, confused, and lost all at the same time. Then on top of it all, while speaking with another doctor for the millionth time, I got the prognosis I never expected.

"I'm sorry but the way your organs are functioning you have about six weeks to live unless you book a series of surgeries to correct the damage."

Even the gauntlet of surgeries wasn't a guarantee. This entire experience was my earthquake. It was the very thing that triggered the tsunami wave of chaos in my life. I thought for sure it would swallow me whole. But it didn't.

Instead it led me to a different path in my life and to a different kind of chaos which I will explain a little later.

Right now, I'm going to pause my story and take you back to the ocean's different wave types. You might have heard of the ocean having rip currents lurking beneath the water's surface that may not be visible from above. What is a rip tide current you might ask? It is a strong, narrow, channel of water that occurs between breaking waves. If you go into the ocean and get caught in a rip current, the forceful channel can rapidly pull you away from the shore and into the depths of the ocean.

What's important to understand is that a rip tide/current is an invisible force that you may not even be aware of. It has the power to pull you under or push you out in the ocean. These are what I call the bad chaos waves, or rip tide chaos. These are the invisible forces around us that we are not aware of. These forces simply add to our chaos. The

8

good news is that small, simple fixes and a sprinkle of awareness, can easily help you get rid of the rip tide chaos.

Let me give you an example. Did you know the type of clothes you wear could be affecting the chaos in your life or the artwork you have on your walls? Believe it or not, a simple picture that you thought looked nice on the wall could be deterring you energetically from achieving your goals.

Sound crazy? Let's say you want to find a loving partner, but you have a painting of a desert on your bedroom wall with a single tree in the middle of the canvas. You thought it looked serene and nice. Simply having that painting in your bedroom and looking at it every day could be keeping you from getting the relationship you want. Why?

Because without even realizing it, you're attracting loneliness into your life. You may think it is serene, but it is a desert … hot … dry … vast … and the tree is the only thing standing out on the canvas. It is alone, as are you. Without even realizing it, you're attracting the very thing you're trying to avoid. This goes deeper than artwork or even the food you choose to eat. The clothes you wear could be contributing to the chaos in your life too, even your hairstyle.

There are four different energy types which I promise to break down for you in a later chapter. It took some exploration, but I came to learn that I am energy type 1. That particular energy type should never wear black or heavy clothing.

Guess what? I had a closet full of black clothes! I had to change things up. I started wearing what is meant for my energy type - colorful, non-symmetric patterns of random structure, and bright clothing. I noticed the effects immediately. It totally changed my energy. I felt more genuine and more authentic and more *me*!

The next day, as I walked into my workplace, I observed the "unspoken but expected norm," where everyone was wearing blues, blacks, and greys. I felt a little anxious standing in my bright flowered blouse and light pink skirt. I knew that people were watching me and possibly even judging me, but I honestly didn't care. One of the managers even came up to me and said "Jothi, you're so daring for wearing bright colors. They do look good on you." I felt really proud of myself for putting myself out there and just being my authentic self.

Why should I wear bland colors just to fit in to this unspoken yet expected "tribe"? For the first time in my life, I realized that I was daring. I brought my authentic self to work and wore what felt good without battling the contagious need to please others.

That shift I made created a ripple effect for my boss and my team. Yes, I'm telling you that adjusting my wardrobe actually impacted not just my work but the dynamic among colleagues. They were curious about my new energy and confidence and wanted to know more.

I told them I was looking into energy profiling and offered to do a quick assessment for each one. Most of my colleagues thought it sounded interesting and let me try. I gave each person the main idea of what kind of clothes they should be wearing, the colors that bring out their particular energy type, and things that really drain their energy type. They took all the information back and started experimenting with it. Well, lo and behold, within a couple weeks, each of them came to me and told me that they could see the difference for themselves.

These simple things, your decor, the food you eat, your clothing, all impact your chaos. But like a rip current, you can't avoid it or do something different unless you know what you're looking for. I know it can feel unsettling and maybe even abrupt sometimes. It is a kind of chaos that can come as a surprise to you. Fear not my friends. You will learn all about it the next few chapters, so you'll be able to spot those rip currents before they pull you out to sea or deep down in the ocean.

So, there's the ugly chaos waves, and the bad chaos waves. Is there such a thing as good chaos waves?

Absolutely.

Good chaos waves are the waves that you want to *invite* in. By now I know you are thinking "Jothi, chaos sounds pretty bad. Why would I ever want to invite chaos into my life?"

Well, as you may have guessed, not all waves are created equal. Therefore, not all chaos is created equal as well.

Let's take a quick look at what I mean by the good chaos waves. Imagine you are sitting near the ocean, watching beautiful foamy waves crash into the shore. A little further out you spot a group of surfers riding high on top of the waves. Each one eventually falls off their board and paddles out to ride the next wave. It looks like a lot of fun.

You decide to join them. As you see a large wave approaching, you gather up enough strength, agility, poise, and balance and start to ride on top of the wave. You feel a rush of adrenaline, energy, and excitement. In that picture-perfect moment, you feel like you are on top of the world. Your heart pounds rapidly. Your eyes are wide. A huge smile crosses your lips as you feel *alive* and purpose driven.

Yet, you also don't really know for sure what's going to happen. The wave could overpower you and knock you off your board. This uncertainty may cause a touch of anxiety or fear, but you ride the wave anyway. You know this is what you were meant to do, and you're all in. You can see the shore is not too far away and you feel the support of the wave and your fellow surfers. You got this, and there's no looking back.

Surfer waves are the waves we chase. They are the perfect blend of excitement and exhilaration with just the right amount of scary. These are the good chaos waves.

Trust me on this. I get I am going against most coaches and gurus when I say this. Yes, we need to strive to get our ocean of life to that early morning state of serenity and peace, but after that it is time to ride those waves.

We cannot allow ourselves to just stay in a peaceful, serene state forever. In fact, if we do, and fail to rise up and reach for the good chaos waves, we will at some point become lazy and comfortable with ourselves. We will slide into an empty-minded state, and catapult back toward bad or even ugly chaos. We must expand our comfort zones and live to think beyond what we believe is possible.

> **"From a state of peace and calmness, you can reach for a state of thriving in life."**
> **– Jothi Dugar**

Let me tell you a little story. I have always been an advocate for female empowerment, especially in cybersecurity and technical fields. When I attended conferences in my field, I noticed that there were hardly any women present. It was a sea of men. I wanted to put myself out there for the world to see. I really wanted to empower myself to have the courage to speak publicly to inspire other women to do the same. I was scared and felt that it would be easier not to go against the norm, but a little voice inside me said, *do it*. If not you, then who else?

Then it happened. A conference coordinator reached out and asked me to present a topic on cyber at their next event. I was excited and nervous. I knew this was my shot to ask for what I really wanted to talk about. I almost wanted to take the "normal" route, play it safe, and just talk about the same topics that every cyber conference has. You know, artificial intelligence, cyber resilience, etc.

But I didn't want to just be another presenter talking about the same old stuff. That would have been the equivalent of jumping off my surfboard and floating back to shore. Instead, as my heart pounded, I said, "I would love to, but I'd prefer to talk about topics I am passionate about and believe are important for the cyber industry." A pause.

"Well, what are you passionate about?"

I slid onto my surfboard, eyeing a wave, and began to paddle. "Empowering women to go into the cyber and technology fields and breaking the glass ceiling of the industry," I replied. The wave was getting closer. It was almost time for me to stand up. Was I about to fall flat on my face?

"Hmm, that does sound different, and interesting. But, you do know your entire audience will probably be male, right?"

At that moment I stood on the surfboard in my mind with confidence. I laughed. "Exactly." I said. And I rode the wave.

I believe after that conversation the conference organizers scrambled to find women who could attend the conference. Despite their efforts, at least 99% of attendees were male. My talk was scheduled to be the last talk of the day and right before happy hour. I don't know what would be worse, the slot before lunch or the slot before happy hour. Who on earth was going to come listen to me talk about empowering women in the workplace when happy hour was right around the corner? I was so tempted to jump off my surfboard and float. I briefly considered bailing on the talk. I could say I was sick and couldn't present but thanks for the opportunity.

Something in me told me I couldn't do that. I was there for a reason. I had to see this through. Instead, I stood in front of the room full of men, put my big girl panties on, and gave it my best shot - sweat running down my dress, and all.

And ... it worked!

About 80% of the conference participants attended my talk. Nearly all of them had tons of questions afterwards. We must have chatted for at least an extra half hour after my session was over. Which means yes, many chose to cut into their happy hour time to stay and speak with me!

"I have a daughter who is interested in cybersecurity, what can I do now to help her break into the field?" someone asked.

It was these kinds of questions that let me know I had done exactly what I was meant to do. Cyber leaders recognized how little they had been doing to advocate for women in the tech field. I felt exhilarated. It was an incredible wave to ride. I would have missed out if I quit before the wave took hold. That is the beauty of good chaos.

Do you now see how our mind, body, and energy work, is congruent with the ocean? The ocean of life within all of us can be peaceful, dangerous, exhilarating, and even destructive. We as humans can choose how we want to ride the different waves of chaos that are constantly within and around us.

Most people believe that any type of chaos is a bad thing, but I hope you can see already that all chaos is not made the same.

**Chaos loves you and you are in the right place at the right time to learn how to love it back.**

Are you ready for real, transformational change in your life? It is time to dive in, my dear. All is well, and you are safe on this journey. Let's ride these waves of chaos together!

## CHAPTER I TOOLKIT

There are three types of chaos in our lives.

- Tsunami chaos is the ugly chaos. It is when a simple external trigger touches on a deep rooted fear/insecurity/vulnerability in your subconscious mind and causes a disproportional reaction from you.
- Rip tide chaos is the bad chaos. This is an invisible force that you may not even be aware of. These forces simply add to our chaos and could be triggered by the clothes you wear, the food you eat, even the decor you have in your home.
- Surfer chaos is the good chaos. This is the exhilarating chaos that inspires you to break past fear and experience the unknown. This is the chaos we strive for and it makes us feel alive.

*Chapter 2*

# DIVING INTO THAT UGLY TSUNAMI CHAOS

*"Understanding the ugly chaos starts by understanding ourselves from within."*
– **Jothi Dugar**

Okay, let's do a quick check-in. How are you feeling? Now that you have a glimpse of the different types of chaos in the ocean of life, think about what wave type you have been encountering the most. Do you float in the serene stillness or find yourself pulled around by unseen forces? Are you at a point in your life where you're riding the surfer waves with exhilaration and awe? Or, are you caught in a tidal wave that pummels your heart and soul over and over again to the point you can't breathe and just want the refuge of the shoreline?

No matter which wave type resonates the most within you right now, I hope you're starting to see that not all chaos is created equal. We're going to explore the biggest, most complex, chaos wave type first. That's right, we're diving right into the tsunami.

A tsunami collects the existing water in the ocean to create the powerful wave of mass destruction.

That means that ugly chaos happens based on decisions you have made and things you choose to do:

Negative thinking.
Labeling yourself.
Self-fulfilling prophecy.
Subconscious blocks.
Fear-based or scarcity thinking.

All of these choices we make contribute to the ugly chaos which then attracts even more ugly chaos until you get to a state of exhaustion and burnout and feel like there is no turning back.

Have you ever felt lost, stuck, and depressed?

I'd be willing to say you might even feel a bit hopeless.

I know it feels like a lot to take on, but the more we examine the ugly chaos, the better we understand it, and the better we understand ourselves from within. Even though ugly chaos can be deep-rooted, almost to our core, there are easy and effective techniques you can enact right away to slowly take you to a state of peace and then to a state of excitement and zest for life.

Remember what I said before, this is not an easy journey, but a necessary one, especially if you really want to live the best life you can possibly live. Understanding the ugly chaos starts by understanding ourselves from within. What do I mean by that? Well, first you need to understand what the mind-body-energy connection is and how it works.

Stay with me.

There are three big parts that make up who you are: your mind, your body, and your energy. Each one is connected to the other. If you change one, you're definitely going to change the other two. When all three work in sync, there is a continuous and harmonious flow between them.

Cue feelings of achievement, excitement, joy, and wonder.

But when we're in a chaos crisis mode, the three parts are not in sync and that's when you start to *feel* the chaos. Most of our ugly chaos starts in our mind. This is why I say we bring ugly chaos onto ourselves. Our mind is powerful. Our thoughts have more influence on us than you can imagine. Think about the saying, "It's all in your head." Well, there is a lot of truth to that. If you think you are a victim, you are right. If you think you are a survivor, you're also right. And, if you think you're a champion, again you're absolutely right.

You may have one friend who is terrified of roller coasters, but you absolutely love the thrill of them. Why does your friend carry that fear around? It could be tied to a bad experience, or nervousness around a fear that she has of lack of control. No matter what the reason, she can choose to decide what her response will be starting with her mind.

Now, I know what you're thinking. Oh c'mon Jothi, do you really want me to believe that I should be in control of my own thoughts, how would I possibly do that? That would drive me insane from having to keep monitoring my thoughts. Well, I promise I won't tell you to "just think happy thoughts and everything will change." However, I do want you to know that the best part of changing and elevating your mindset is that *you are in total control* of the whole process.

**If you do not stand guard as the gatekeepers of your own mind, who will?**

You didn't ask for this power, I get it. I know it is a lot easier to blame things on others and make them do something about changing your thoughts, feelings, and emotions. But guess what, you choose your thoughts. You do happy. You do excitement. You also do victim mentality, depression, anxiety, or any other so called "negative" thoughts. Yes, you do have a choice in all of this.

Thoughts don't happen *to* you. You are in charge of them. All of them.

Let's say that you have a disagreement with a colleague one day, and you didn't fully resolve the situation, process it, and release it from your mind. That thought or feeling keeps lingering inside you, swirling around. You keep thinking of what you could have or should have said.

You start thinking, how dare he say that to me, and create a whole story about how he must have not been raised well, or he must have a big ego. Soon, just the thought of him makes you annoyed and angry. You've already labeled him in your mind as "the enemy." Okay, maybe you're not that hostile, but your mind definitely attached a "bad" label to this person.

You feel that you are totally in the right for feeling this way because he exhibits behaviors that set you off. You start complaining to your friends about this person. You may even blame him for some things going wrong in your own life. It is so much easier to look outward and say "hey, this person/place/thing is the reason I have these problems."

Why? Because, by waiting for him to do or say something to make you feel better, you can avoid having to look within, to see what you haven't resolved for yourself. To make matters worse, there is something within *you* that is *attracting* this person or the way he's acting *towards* you.

By waiting for him to do something, you're giving your power away. You're putting it in someone else's hands to change the chaos that is going on within *you*. And, who is responsible for *you?* You and only you have the power to experience life in any way, shape, or form that you choose to. You're in charge, no one, place, or thing else. And it all starts by understanding your mind.

Now, when I say mind, I'm talking about the two main parts of the mind at a high level. This is not a biology or medical class or book, so I will not be going deep into all the different parts of our brain here. But there are two main parts that I want you to become aware of - the conscious mind, and the subconscious mind. If you're anything like me, sometimes both these parts seem at war with each other.

Let me make a quick point here. Feelings and emotions may seem controllable, but they truly aren't. Emotions are irrational. They are not meant to make "sense" in your mind. That is why someone may seem to behave irrationally by getting "emotional" about something that seems rather frivolous. That is because emotions happen *to* us, and it is ok to have those tears come flowing in out of the blue when you least expect them, or feel angry about something that happened to someone else.

However, *acting* on those emotions is where your true power lies. Just because you feel angry, does not mean you need to act out in anger on the other person. Just because you feel sad and hurt, does not mean you need to act out with resentment and harshness to someone. Your power lies in your ability to *respond* to the situation regardless of what your exterior world of people, places, events, things, and situations throw at you.

We will journey through a whole chapter on tactics for combating ugly chaos in the mind and marry the conscious with the subconscious. But right now, I'd like to talk briefly about the body part of the mind-body-energy connection. This is the connection that often goes amiss.

Let's say you've been having a dull pain in your stomach for a while. The first course of action, if concerned, is to reach out to your doctor for help. Therefore, you visit your doctor and he immediately prescribes a medication to subdue your physical pain. The pain seems to go away temporarily. All good right?

Well, not exactly. Did the doctor try to find out the root cause of the pain? Did he ask if you have been having any emotional or mental anguish, trauma, or changes lately? Did he make any sort of connection between how you've been *feeling* and the physical symptoms?

As you can probably guess, the average Western medicine doctor does not try to identify or solve the root cause of the problem. Instead they treat the symptom. Your stomach issue could be stemming from your emotions. Where is the magic pill for that? (No, anti-anxiety and antidepressants do not count. Once again, they only treat the symptom).

When we don't process our feelings and find a way to release them naturally, they can manifest as physical means throughout your body. Sadness, grief, anger, resentment, loneliness are all feelings that can cause chaos in your body. Your body responds by activating pain receptors. What it is really saying is, "hey you, something isn't right here and needs to be addressed." And, the more medications you take to subdue your symptoms, the more you are asking your body to mask your root cause issues, which will keep getting worse.

Let's pause here and return to my story. I had just been told I had six weeks to live unless I went under the knife for a series of experimental and exploratory surgeries. As I sat on my bed, in pain, asking the universe what is it that I needed to do, I prayed for the answers to come to me. Then one day, I had an epiphany. I needed to heal for myself. There had to be a way.

Naturally, I did what every person does when they seek an answer and receive something vague in return. I ignored it. I figured something clearer would come along. I waited for a few days. Nothing came.

Finally, on the fifth day, with as much strength as I could muster, I got up and planted myself in front of the computer. It was time to take action and find an answer from the best resource that I knew: Mr. Google.

I listened to my intuition and knew that my body needed something natural to heal. I just wasn't sure what it was. I set my intention to allow myself to heal naturally, and the answers would come to me. Deep within my heart, I knew there had to be an *alternative* to whatever the confused doctors thought. I no longer wanted to be a medical mystery with a mess of insides.

Most of the time when you look for answers, the answers will come. I was scared. I knew my body could not tolerate more surgeries. I didn't want to die. I couldn't turn my head without my body radiating in pain. No amount of pain medication was going to fix the root of my problem.

In fact, the pain medication caused ulcers on top of the existing issues I had for which I was prescribed even more medicine!

I set my intention and my determination to heal myself naturally, and that was that. I started looking frantically on for natural remedies to address each of my physical symptoms, day in and day out. My friends, my family, and my colleagues all thought I was crazy. "Jothi, the doctors gave you six weeks to live, what are you waiting for? Just get the surgeries," they said.

I went to the surgeon I somewhat trusted and told him that I was going find another way. Just to be safe, I booked my plan B - to get the first surgery six weeks out. Maybe it was to ease my loved ones' fears about the possibility of losing me. Maybe it was to calm everyone down. Maybe it was so I had a second chance if my quest for natural modalities came up empty.

But deep down, I was determined. There was no Plan B in my mind.

"I will find a natural fix for these hernias and get all my organs back in the right areas within six weeks," I affirmed to myself with resolute determination every day. Of course the surgeon blatantly laughed at my face and told me "Good luck with that. We'll see you in six weeks."

Who was I, this leader in cyber and mom to three kids, to say I could heal myself, when a medical professional that spent years in med school told me the contrary? Well, what I had that he didn't, was my own intention and willpower. I was a woman on a mission. I would find a way to naturally treat the root of my problems, not just the superficial symptoms. I wanted to live. And, that was that.

I will share more of my journey in the next few chapters, but for now I would like to circle back to the last segment of our mind-body-energy connection: energy. Now, energy is a word thrown around in many different ways. You have the science and technology energy. You have the "woo woo" wellness world energy. Some people think energy is this invisible "thing" you feel. Others think energy is this intangible thing we need. Have you ever said, "I need more energy?" Or have you looked at a younger person and say, "Where do you get so much energy from?"

Energy may seem like a mystical thing. Imagine walking into a corporate or technical setting and suggesting everyone examine their inner energy. You're going to get a lot of raised eyebrows and perhaps a few dissenting chuckles. The wellness world seems like just that: a totally different world to analytical and technology driven left brained folks. The funny thing is that many people in the wellness world consider the realm of technology to be an entirely different world to them too! What if there was a way to merge these worlds that feel so far apart?

Most of us do not understand that at the very core essence that's at the heart of everything, every object, every living creature, is energy. When you boil everything down to the smallest level, it boils down to a form of energy.

In living creatures this energy is otherwise known as our life force energy, qi, prana, etc. If we don't understand how our energy works and how it's connected to our mind and body, we can be inadvertently adding more chaos to our lives and to others.

I think a great, but simple way to illustrate the energy connection for this part of our journey together, is this example. Imagine you are out shopping, and you see a piece of clothing you really like. You're attracted to the color, the pattern, maybe even the texture. One may argue this is simply a manifestation of your fashion sense, but it is much more than that. The truth is that you are resonating at the same vibrational frequency as that piece of clothing. You're attracted to it for a reason beyond finding it visually pleasing.

The same thing happens with people. You can feel when your energy is in sync with another person. This is how best friends and romantic partners find each other. Of course, there are people who are on a different frequency than you. You may be higher or lower, and conflict can arise. Think back to that colleague that gets on your nerves. You're probably operating on two different frequency levels.

The goal is to become aware of our own energy, the energy surrounding us, and not be scared of it being "woo woo." If you learn how your energy not only affects yourself, but others, you will also learn to recognize how the energy of your surroundings, people, places, things, affect you and either harmonize the chaos, or adds to your chaos.

The mind-body-energy connection is a beautifully complex thing. But simply put, if you let things go on too long in your mind, it is going to affect your body. The same goes for your energy. These three different parts are all connected and if one starts moving, they all start moving.

How are you doing at this very moment? Pause for a moment and check in with yourself.

What are your thoughts telling you?

How does your body feel?

Can you perceive the energy of the people, places, and things, around you? (It is there, but can you sense it yet?)

When you are ready, we're going to go deep into the ugly chaos in your mind, and boy do I have lots of tools that you will be adding to your toolkit.

You're on your way, my friend. You're doing this!

## CHAPTER 2 TOOLKIT

- Ugly chaos can attract more chaos until you reach a state of exhaustion and burnout if it is not recognized, processed, then released from your Ocean of Life.
- There are three big parts that make up who you are: your mind, your body, and your energy. Each one is connected to the other. If you change one, you're definitely going to change the other two.
- A large percentage of our ugly chaos starts in our mind.
- When we don't process our feelings and find a way to release them naturally, they can manifest through physical means in your body. Sadness, grief, anger, resentment, loneliness. All these feelings can cause chaos in your body.
- The very core essence that's at the heart of everything, every object, every living creature is energy. If we don't understand how our energy works and how it's connected to our mind and body, we can be inadvertently adding more chaos to our lives and to others.

*Chapter 3*

# THE TSUNAMI CHAOS
# IN YOUR MIND

*Everything in life is happening for you, because life has prepared you for this moment. You are now ready to conquer this challenge to move on to your next level in the game of life*
**– Jothi Dugar**

I know the wellness world can seem daunting. Especially to those in the corporate ecosystem. If you work in certain fields such as IT, cyber, or technology, it might seem like there are too many wellness options out there. Mindful meditation. Visualization. Breathing exercises. Gratitude journaling. Are you tired of too many people telling you what to do? I mean, it does take a little bit of time to sort through all the suggestions and figure out what works best for *you*. It can all seem very confusing to a person who already has so much going on in his or her own life.

Like you.

Fear not.

By the end of this chapter, you are going to learn simple, easy, and effective ways to use *your own mind* to change your destiny and manage the chaos in your life. First, I need you to read this carefully:

**The power is already within you.**

Read it again. Okay, now I'm going to teach you how to become aware of your power and then magnify it.

Let's talk about mindset for a second. I define mindset as the ability you have to choose how you want to set your mind amidst the chaos. Mindset is a choice, a skill, an art, and a science! Transforming, or should I say rewiring, your mindset can be learned.

Everything you do is related. Remember our mind-body-energy connection? This is just like that. Your thoughts affect your actions which then affects your behavior. The more you allow negative thoughts to roll in, and you take the additional step of acting on those negative thoughts, you have now started a habit of negative behavior. All of these have an impact on your body and energy. Because at the end of the day, *everything* is a form of energy.

Everything starts with your thoughts. I mean everything. But that doesn't mean you have to only think positive thoughts. No one can do that. It is not even normal! Even though everything starts with your thoughts, it really just means you need to become the palace guardian of your thoughts with the palace being your mind. You as the palace guardian need to decipher which of those thoughts are allowed into your palace, and which ones are sent to the long lost galaxy far far away.

Believe it or not, you have the ability to transform your thoughts. Now, notice I said transform, not *change* your thoughts. This is very important. You want your thoughts to undergo an evolution. You do not want to simply switch from negative to positive. Do you accept the bold truth that you can *choose* how to set your mind when there is all this chaos going on within and around you?

I know you're giving me a weak, maybe a mediocre "eh" right now.

That is ok.

Just like any other skill in your life, the more you become aware of, the more it peaks your curiosity, and the more you're curious, the more you want to learn.

Then, practice, practice, practice, and the better you get.

So I said the very first step in choosing how to set your mind is awareness. That has a lot to do with becoming aware of how you manage your expectations.

What expectations do you have of yourself?
What about others?
Think of a time when your expectations were not met.
How did you feel?
What was going on in your life at that time?
I bet you felt disappointed, stressed, maybe even a little angry.

I have always been a go-getter. As I worked my way up to become a leader in the Cyber industry, I often fell prey to my own expectations. They were enormous. I felt that I had to be perfect. I had to hide my emotions so I wouldn't be seen as weak. I stifled so much of my authentic self to fit into the boxes I thought others wanted me to sit inside. I had this image in my head of who I thought I had to be and who I had to look like to be taken seriously. But it wasn't me. Some parts were me, but it wasn't 100 percent me.

It took time, but eventually I broke down my own personal expectations of myself one by one. I was a woman, but it was okay to show vulnerability and let emotions shine through. By leading with vulnerability, I was more trustworthy and *real*. I wasn't weak, I was approachable. I wasn't emotional, I was authentic. I had to stop adding so much pressure to myself. I began to realize that the expectations I chose to put on myself and others played a significant role in contributing to the ugly chaos in my ocean of life. My expectations were leading to *unnecessary stress*.

## THE TORNADO OF CHAOS

If you are anything like me (at least the old me), you are probably connected to your work 24/7. You get up every day and the first thing you do is check your phone, right? You are working more than 40 hours a week because the office and the world can't survive without you, in your mind. You might be struggling with sleep because you're always wired and on the go. I'm even taking a wild guess that you are not prioritizing your own personal health and wellness. At some point when you're smack in the middle of the tornado of chaos, you resort to having low morale and low energy.

Does this sound anything like you?

Well, guess what? I was no exception either.

Welcome to the tornado of chaos my friend. Think a moment about how the tornado of chaos manifests in your own life. Are you emotional for no apparent reason sometimes? Are you wondering if you're in the right job or what your actual purpose in life is? Do you feel like you're so tired but just can't get yourself to have some downtime for yourself to recharge? Has your marriage or relationship taken a turn for the worse, and you have no idea what happened? Well, if you answered a resounding *yes* to one or more of these, then you guessed it. You're in the eye of the tornado of chaos! Congratulations!

Now, I know, I know. You're about the close this book and think this is some woo woo, shi shi, foo foo, whatever else you want to call it type of book where I'm just going to tell you all is well and just go with the flow dear.

Trust me, I am not making light of this situation by any means. In fact, I know exactly how you feel. Why the heck would I be happy about being in the eye of a tornado, especially when its name is Chaos?

I know this may *feel* impossible to do or even consider, but please hang with me on this one when I say there is *always* a gift in every situation. So guess what? You now are at least *aware* of the tornado of chaos swirling around you and within you. Before, you were living your life by default and unconscious of all the chaos that may have been swirling inside you or another person in your close circle. And now, you're conscious of it. That's a great first step on your journey!

I know it seems like there is no light at the end of the tunnel and the tunnel feels long. That's okay. Let's take a pause and look at a tool from the book *Ask and it's Given,* by Ester Hicks. It is called The Emotional Guidance Scale.

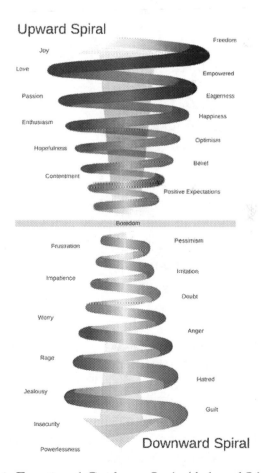

Figure 1: Emotional Guidance Scale (Ask and It's Given by Ester Hicks and Jerry Hicks)

The top is the "upward" spiral which lists the positive emotions. The "downward" spiral lists the negative emotions. That grey line represents the calm, serene ocean, with no waves of chaos. This is the state that most people feel they need to strive to be in. The feelings in the downward spiral below this gray line represent when we choose to set our minds to a state of low vibration. How do you know when you're functioning at a low vibrational level?

Well, ask yourself, how do I feel right now? Do I feel good or kind of crummy? If you feel crummy, then you're starting to go in the downward spiral. This is where ugly chaos magnifies within us. The problem with ugly chaos is that once you start going downwards in the spiral, you have to *consciously* realize what is happening in order for you to move back up. Otherwise, remember how a tsunami works? If you don't control the impact that the trigger has on your ocean of life, it's going to come rearing its ugly head with a vengeance. This causes you to go deeper in the downward spiral, which then makes it harder and harder for you to come back up.

The feelings on the upward spiral above the gray line are where we can truly move beyond the waveless state of peace in our ocean of life and expand into that surfer chaos. This is where we can find our bliss, passion, and excitement. This is where you really want to be in life! It's not just in a waveless, calmness, living in your comfort zone state-of-mind. You want to be surfing those waves of chaos, feeling excited, passionate, and exuberant in life!

So, when you're in a state of despair, way down in the tsunami chaos, how do you move up into the surfer chaos state quickly?

Short answer is, you *don't*.

This is the number one mistake that people make. I know it's very tempting to try and jump from a feeling of despair to a feeling of bliss too quickly and expect that bliss to stick. But, when it doesn't happen, how do you feel? You'll feel even more crummy and maybe even agitated which then will cause you to dive into an even further state of ugly chaos in the downward spiral of emotions.

If you keep trying even harder to jump to a much higher state too quickly, too soon, you'll just fall back down even faster. Now you're entering the dreaded tsunami state. It's a pretty vicious cycle, right? Well my friends, it's not all dismal and gloomy. I have good news. There are a bunch of great tools you can use in your daily life to prevent this from happening! In fact, I'd like to share one with you right now.

Let's take a look at the Step Ladder tool that I created for you.

## CHAOS TOOL 1: THE STEP LADDER

Picture this, you're deep in the tornado of chaos. You're swirling around the downward spiral of discomfort. It feels like you're in an actual tornado. There is no end in sight. You're feeling heavy-hearted, tired, exhausted, and just feel like there's a dark heavy cloud hanging over your head. You wish you could just jump up to the upward spiral into a state of calmness and peace at least, but you just can't seem to get there. In comes the Chaos Step Ladder tool!

When you're so far down the downward spiral, your number one goal is to become aware of your current state and the feelings around it *without* judgement, blame, ridicule, or criticism of yourself or others. The second goal is simply to try get your state one step further up in your emotional ladder.

Let me repeat that. *One step* further up. Not ten, not five, not all the way up. Just *one*. Let's talk about expectations again. When you start going on a downward spiral, ask yourself:

*Am I in this downward spiral because I had some expectations that were not being met by others for me?*

*Am I here because I set my expectations on something or someone and judging them based on my own expectations?*

*Did I expect them or the situation to meet my expectations exactly as I set them?*

*Did I choose to stay in a low vibrational state and label myself as the victim when my expectations weren't met?*

Yup, I get it. I know it's tough to look at things this way and it's much easier to *choose* to be mad or angry and leave the work to someone else to bring you up the ladder. But guess who has the power then? Not just any power, *your power*. Why would you *ever* want to give *your* power to someone else like that?

Maybe you expected things to happen and they didn't happen the way you expected. Maybe someone wronged you and you feel completely blindsided. Maybe someone abused you and they totally deserve all your scorn.

I know it's hard sometimes to feel this way, and I'm by no means making light of any trauma or abusive situation here. I know I have been through my own share of trauma myself and still believe in this saying.

> *Everything in your life is happening for you, and it's your job to find that gift in every situation or circumstance. Life is always preparing you for the next big challenge, so if you're undergoing a challenge right now, congratulations! You are ready for this, and everything you have learned so far has prepared you for this moment.*

A lot of our chaos stems from expectations. As living, breathing, beings it is hard to navigate the world without some sort of expectation. We're wired for expectation. But when things don't go the way we hope, we feel triggered. Let me explain.

When I was feeling upset and vulnerable after my third baby was born and I was put in this horrific, dire situation by my OB, I expected my husband to do a lot of things for me. I expected him to be supportive, encouraging, loving and kind emotionally, mentally, and physically. In my head, it was a given. But he wasn't, or so I thought as I sat on my bed in pain wondering why he hasn't checked on me to see how I was doing.

Turns out, my husband *was* all these things, in his own way. He was trying his best to keep our two older kids occupied and entertained. He was helping bring my food upstairs since I couldn't even move. He was shuffling the kids to and from school. He was trying to manage the household and run errands and do the groceries. He was available if I needed him to take me to doctor or therapist appointments. Yes, he wasn't emotionally available the way I expected him to be, but he was trying his best to be supportive from his point of view with the skills, tools, and knowledge that he had at the time.

Instead of discounting his efforts and choosing to feel sad, alone, uncared for, and upset, I chose to release the tsunami chaos from my mind. I did not want to choose to play the role of a *victim*. I had to change my perspective and see his efforts through a different set of goggles. The love goggles gave me a more loving and unconditional compassionate view of the same situation and circumstances, a view where I had the power within me to dissipate and diminish my disappointment and agitation.

I knew I couldn't rush it as I was trying to heal myself and I knew this was a process and a marathon, not a sprint. I took it one day at a time. If I only moved up one step in the ladder the whole day, that was progress. I could be my harshest critic sometimes, as I know some of you can be too. There was no point in blaming me or him in this process. I once heard Stacy Martino, a relationship expert talk about *blame* as "*being lame*", and I definitely did not want to *be lame*.

So, let's talk about you now. Let's say you come home from a tiring day of work, and you're really fed up dealing with an issue in your job. What you could really use right now is a hug from your husband, out of anyone else in the world. But turns out your husband also had a rough day, and just wants to be by himself right now. What emotions do you choose to feel? Do you act on your negative emotions or do you allow yourself to process them first?

Do you feel forgotten, angry, or disappointed? Maybe your husband sends you a nice text before he goes to bed to check on you. You're still in need of some physical connection that makes you feel warm, safe, and protected, right? So, yes he did actually show you affection, but it wasn't the kind of affection you were expecting. Does that mean that it can't have the same effect on you? You see how your expectations can stir up the ugly chaos?

What if the next time something like this happens, you read his text message and you visualize a hug from him and just allow yourself to really feel the same feelings you would feel if he had given you a physical hug? You don't think it would be the same? Try it.

Your brain is not as "smart" as you think it is. It cannot tell the difference between what is physical reality and what is virtual reality. So, by allowing yourself to visualize a hug from your husband and choosing to feel the same connection as you would have felt if did give you a physical hug, your mind, body, and energy would feel the exact same way in your subconscious mind.

So, once you've identified your expectations vs. reality, you can see through the eye of the tornado of chaos a little clearer. Take a look at your step ladder. If you manage your expectations and allow yourself to use a different lens to see things from a new perspective, do you think you can move just one step up on your step ladder?

If you didn't receive that hug, but you did receive a nice note, can you use your own inner power of your mind to help you feel loved and cherished? Manage your expectations in the equation. Take his loving text for what it is, a kind and caring gesture. Now, can you allow yourself to feel a little lighter? Perhaps instead of angry, you can feel calm. Or, instead of resentful you feel only slightly angry. Each increment up the ladder is an improvement. Remember, you've conditioned yourself all these years to a certain mindset, and now you're rewiring your mindset and your holistic operating system. You didn't get here overnight, so don't add undue chaos by expecting things to change overnight, either.

The Step Ladder Tool is all about awareness, managing expectations, and then recognizing the ways you can change your mindset in tiny little ways. That will help you move up the ladder and into a state of bliss and excitement slowly yet steadily. With each step, your tornado of chaos gets a little bit smaller and a little less destructive. My friends, take baby steps. One step at a time.

## STRATEGIES TO MOVE UP STEP BY STEP

I know what you're thinking. Jothi, really? Just manage my expectations and I'll get happier? That is not what I'm saying. I promise. I just want you to become aware of your expectations and how they can affect the ugly chaos in your mind. This is just the first step.

One way you can move upward in the spiral of emotions is by allowing yourself to feel grateful. It is literally the easiest and fastest way to move up each step. I invite you to try the Gratitude 100 List Tool.

Grab a notepad and pen. Yes I know, I am old school for a purpose. *Do not* do this on the computer. If you have a new journal, even better. Call it your gratitude journal and use a new and fresh pen to write out 20 things you are grateful for.

There is a science behind manually writing things on paper. A transfer of energy occurs from your pen to the paper. It gives you instant gratification just by writing it out and feeling those feelings inside. It is *not* the same when you type things on a computer.

You can't seem to think of a 20 things? Go big and go small. They can be people, situations, events, ideas, actions, knowledge, skills, viewpoints, dreams, weather conditions, environments, food, housing, your body, mind, any parts of your mind-body-spirit connection, music, activities, the fact you are alive, hobbies, passions, and whatever else you can think of that you are grateful for. 20 things. You can do it.

Once you have your list, take a picture of it with your phone and keep it handy. Take that list with you wherever you go. Look at your list and say out loud (if you can) or in your mind the following: *I am truly grateful for/that …"* Do this for at least 5 items on your list. More importantly, *feel* the feelings deep inside as you imagine these things. Allow the feelings to come in. If you feel emotional, it is okay. It is working. Feel them in your heart and hold them there.

Do this when you first wake up in the morning. Do this when you go to bed at night. And do this if you're feeling stressed or overwhelmed or feel as if you are sinking lower into the downward spiral. As you come up with more items, keep adding them to your list. My challenge for you, my friends, is to reach at least 100 items over the course of 30 days. Mark it on your calendar. You will be so surprised how many things will come to you when you're seeking something, and really looking for them using your new gratitude goggles.

Need another tool to move upwards in your positive spiral? Practice the art of thanking others, even for the smallest action they may have taken. Tell them you are thankful for their action. Then it down on your list!

For self-gratitude, another exercise you can do is look in the mirror and take a long, deep, look at your beautiful reflection. Think about your organs, cells, and all the parts that make up your ocean of life. Thank each one. "Thank you, eyes for showing me beautiful things." "Thank you nose, for allowing me to smell all different scents." Write them on your list.

I know. I know. This whole gratitude thing might feel silly. Or maybe I just gave you yet ANOTHER to-do on your list. But let's really dig deep and look at things for what they truly are. Why should I feel grateful for my arm?

Well, if I didn't have my arm, would that add to my ugly chaos in my ocean of life? If the answer is yes, then why wouldn't you feel grateful for having that arm? You see? The more we allow ourselves to feel grateful for every little thing, the more we send energetic vibrations into the universe. Guess what? The universe rebounds those vibrations right back at us by sending us more things to be grateful for. How cool is that?

It is a win-win. Yet some of us find it really hard to allow ourselves to feel grateful. I get it. It is so much easier than it seems sometimes. If you're finding this difficult, it might be due to some deep core level trauma or pain you need to release. In that case, I would highly urge you to book an Integrated Intuitive Energy Healing session with me.

Check my website www.jothidugar.com and book a Chaos Clarity call, and we'll work together to come up with deeper support for you.

I know everyone is on a different path, at different levels, and need different levels of support. So, if you feel like you need a deeper level of support, encouragement, and boost to your operating system, I am here for you. Just a call away!

# SHINING YOUR LIGHT FOR OTHERS

Another tool I have for you is called the Shining Your Light Tool. When you find yourself on the downward spiral of feelings, I bet the last thing you want to do is try to be there for someone else. I bet you're exhausted and the mere thought of trying to help someone when you feel like you're drowning is overwhelming. I get it. What if I told you that being there for someone else is one of the quickest ways to not only raise the vibration of the person you're helping, but also your own?

By helping others with something big or small, you raise the cortisol levels within you, which will help you to feel good inside. There is a light within you. Their gratitude and your sense of purpose unite to take your mind/thoughts/energy away from what was causing your state to go downward to begin with.

Hold the door for a stranger. Compliment someone's shirt. Call a friend you haven't heard from in a while. Pay for the drive thru order behind you. That tiny effort will go a long way into raising you from one state to the next. You can go from bitter to calm or devastated to sad. Remember, the goal is to move up the spiral *one step at a time*. I used to try to jump states too quickly. If I felt hopeless or lost, not knowing if I would make it out of my situation, I'd try to force myself to get to happiness rapidly. I thought I had to always be positive and optimistic. And, guess what? It never worked.

I have read a lot of self-help books, done a lot of expensive programs, and followed a lot of self-help gurus out there. I tried to stay positive and do the affirmations. I have tried everything that wellness gurus had to offer. I think I've done every possible personal development, relationship development, leadership, healing, and wellness program that ever existed. I tried so hard. When a technique "failed me" I wanted to give up. I felt worse than I had before I started.

It took time, but I learned I had to take a step back and recognize sometimes I had to slow down to speed up. I needed to be okay with taking one step at a time and learn the art of feeling grateful. When

I was in excruciating pain from the baby, I decided to go on a deep, exploratory journey to find holistic and natural modalities to heal me before my onslaught of additional surgeries were scheduled. I was in my own tornado of chaos. I couldn't figure out how I could possibly help others since I couldn't even move without pain. I felt useless.

Then I realized something. My two older kids who I hadn't been around much, just wanted to be around me. That was all they hoped for. They wanted to feel that I was with them, even if I couldn't physically do a lot. Instead of feeling guilty about not being able to spend much time with them, or do activities with them, I called them into my bedroom. I told them I couldn't move much, but hey I'm still here, alive and alert, so I can surely read stories to them, chat with them about their day, and could still give them a hug as long as they came right next to me.

That's all they wanted. They knew mommy was in pain. They didn't care what I did with them, as long as I was just with them. It didn't take me long to start forgetting about my own pain and climb up that ladder quicker and quicker. The more I allowed myself to be there for my kids, the faster I went up my spiral and felt better emotionally, which then helped me feel better physically too.

> **Big moments don't lead to massive impact. Cherish and celebrate the millions of small moments and small wins that will lead you to the big moments.**
> **- Jothi Dugar**

# CHAOS TOOL 2: RIPPLES OF GRIEF

Quiz time!

What are the three chaos wave types? Do you remember? That's right, good chaos, rip tide chaos, and tsunami chaos. Just like there are chaos wave types, there are also grief wave types. I call them the ripples of grief. Grief gets a bad rap, as it is considered bad to grieve. I mean let's face it. Grief is sad. We don't talk about it much and people pass judgements on what is the appropriate amount of time to grieve.

My definition for grief is this: ***The normal process of responding to a feeling of loss that we must go through to enable us to move upwards in the tornado of chaos.***

My friends, grief is a normal process. It is a normal response to loss. We have to go through it. We can't avoid it. Once we allow it in, process it, then release it, we'll move up to happier and more positive states of being. First thing is first. We must allow ourselves to experience all the ripples of grief, perhaps even multiple times, to truly process the emotions and feelings that arise from the loss we've experienced. Avoiding these ripples just means more obstacles in the future. Trust me.

The major grief ripples include denial & isolation, anger, depression, bargaining, and acceptance. I am sure there are other grief ripples you've experienced beyond the ones I've just listed. That is okay. We're just going to focus on these for now. Everyone's grief journey is different. Sometimes you process through the ripples step by step in order. Other times, you develop ripples within ripples and can bounce between two steps. No matter what, trust that whatever you are feeling is 100 percent okay.

It is also okay to grieve *anything* you may consider a loss. Yes, anything at all. People are the most common. But you can grieve the loss of a job, or a friendship, or an event that did not happen. I know during the COVID-19 pandemic, people are grieving the loss of their freedom and socialization time. You can grieve a decision you made or didn't make. You can even grieve something that you wish you said, or did, or didn't say or do. Just remember that grieving is normal and any topic is fair game.

Also, friends, I want you to know that it is healthy to move in whatever speed you wish, between whichever ripples you want. However there is one very important secret to know. *You need to keep moving.* Use your Step Ladder Tool to find ways to move yourself one step at a time upwards in the tornado of chaos. Remember, they are ripples of grief for a reason. Ripples are not stationary. They start at a center and undulate outward. Keep those ripples moving. Don't block their energy. I tried. It doesn't work.

As an overachiever, perfectionist, and a society-proclaimed super woman, I wanted to do it all. I had to do it all, or so I told myself. I wanted to be there for everyone. I needed to be everything to my kids, my husband, my team, my job, and my organization. When I dropped the ball on something, I thought I was a failure. When I missed my daughter's Kindergarten graduation because I was at home in excruciating pain, I thought I was a bad mom. The ripples of grief washed over me. But I ignored them. I felt like it was weak to grieve when no one had passed away. I was scared. I didn't want to be labeled with a medical diagnosis like depression. Still, I continued to put a lot of pressure on myself to be supermom and be there for everyone and everything. Did I mention I'm a perfectionist? Where are all my perfectionist friends at? I see you!

When I was nearly immobile after that fateful third c-section, I had so many questions.

*Why me?*
*Why did the OB cause so much chaos to my body?*
*What is the point of all of this?*

I wanted that perfectionist validation. I hunted down that golden answer as to why everything was happening. But that is not what I received. No, instead I learned the OB was not in the right frame of mind when she performed that c-section. She was burnt out and my health was a byproduct of that.

"Did I do that?" she said as she gave me a perplexed look seeing my incision.

"Hmm maybe the table was tilted, or sometimes the scapula just runs off on its own." she said as I sat there trying hard not to throw my shoe at her.

When I didn't get the justification or answers that made sense to my questions as to why this happened to me, I crashed deep into the bottom layers of the tornado of chaos. I could barely move. I couldn't attend any of my kids' events. I couldn't go to social activities or even leave my house much. I couldn't hold my newborn baby except when I was sitting on the bed and needed to hand her off when she was done nursing. I was always a very active person. I never sat in one place for too long.

But there I was. Stationary. Resentful. Feeling alone. Needing to grieve the loss of so many things that I wanted to do but couldn't. The more I pushed down my loss and grief, the worse I felt. I knew that I had to stare at my ripples of grief head on, feel the feelings, let the ripples wash through my ocean of life. Only then would I be able to move forward.

I took one day at a time and just allowed myself to cry it out. I let it all go. I felt the feelings, enhanced my faith, and trust in the universe that I was going to heal myself. I set my intention to heal no matter what. I honored each situation for what it was and sent my love to them. Then, I let them go from my internal human operating system. I knew suppressing them and repressing my feelings was only damaging my body even more.

My hope is that you don't have to experience a catastrophic event to realize this. I hope you take this tool to heart. Use it! Don't push grief away because it will ripple back with a vengeance.

## CHAOS TOOL 3: CHAOS OF THOUGHTS

Are you still with me? I know this is heavy stuff. We're getting deeper and deeper. If you feel uncomfortable, I challenge you to sit with that discomfort. If you're feeling uneasy, take a moment and try to pinpoint where that anxiety is coming from. When you're ready, let's dive into my third and final tool for releasing ugly chaos of the mind. Let's talk about the chaos of thoughts.

Quick recap. We learned that our thoughts become our beliefs that lead to our actions. Our actions then affect our behavior and lead to habits, right? So how do we transform our thoughts? I mean, we get thousands of thoughts coming in and going out of our minds on a minute by minute basis. How can we grab them and examine them?

Well, take those thousands of thoughts and create two buckets that every single thought will fit into. One bucket is EmPower Thoughts. The other is Dis-EmPower thoughts. Every thought fits into one of these buckets. Here's how.

EmPower thoughts build you up. These are the thoughts that make you feel good. They enable you to move upwards in the emotional spiral. These thoughts keep the power within you. You don't hand your power to anyone else by having these thoughts. Look at the word Empower. Think of it as "Power in Me". When you process Em-Powering thoughts, you keep your power within you which then powers you up.

Dis-EmPower thoughts make you feel, you guessed it, bad, crummy, or negative. These thoughts push you downward in the emotional spiral and quite possibly push others downward as well. You may assume that thinking negatively of others as much as you feel justified in doing so will make you feel better within yourself, think back to all the times you had this false assumption and executed it. Did thinking negative of another person regardless of how much they have wronged you make you feel happy, and joyful inside?

Dis-EmPower thoughts are exactly what the compound words

mean. They "dis" or remove your power. They force you to hand your power over to others in your external world as you are expecting change in action/words from someone else to enable you to feel good within your internal world.

EmPower thoughts start with sticking with the facts. If you had an expectation and some part of it was met, your EmPower thoughts are the ones that say "hey, I'm grateful that this one thing happened." Having positive expectations, choosing to look at the person or situation holistically (not just what appears to be in the moment), having positive assumptions, taking personal responsibility for yourself and your own actions are all EmPower thoughts.

These are also the thoughts you use your gratitude goggles for a perspective shift. Can you look at things using a creative frame of mind? Is there something you can do to navigate the situation in a positive, uplifting, and empowering way? Can you think of a EmPower thought right now? I bet you can!

Dis-EmPower thoughts are rooted in "all or nothing" thinking. These are catastrophizing thoughts. You know what I'm talking about right? Your wife doesn't come home on time, and you immediately jump to wild conclusions as to what could have happened to her? Your mind races. Your anxiety tries to offer you some sort of control by fortune telling. You start thinking about how she must have forgotten about your special plans "again." You start to think about how she purposely stayed out late just to spite you. We've all been there. I know, these kinds of thoughts don't sound logical or maybe even rational. They discount any positivity. They over generalize. I must warn you. If you don't take control over your mind starting with your thoughts, no one else will. "So what do I do?" you wonder.

Well, first, observe for a week what types of thoughts are coming through daily. I want you to observe without judgement or criticism of yourself. Do not try to change anything. Write down at the end of the day what percentage of your thoughts were EmPower thoughts and

Dis-EmPower thoughts. I know, I know, it sounds like a ton of work. But it gets easier, I promise!

Now, after completing step one, I want you to take notice of your thoughts and start telling yourself as they come in "EmPower thought" or "Dis-EmPower thought." If it is an EmPower thought, give yourself kudos and try to bring in two more EmPower thoughts. For example, let's say you're walking outside and think "Wow, it is a beautiful day outside!" That is an EmPower thought! Can you bring to life two additional EmPower thoughts? Invite those thoughts in. But Jothi, what if it is a Dis-EmPower thought?

I got you. If it is a Dis-EmPower thought, again, do not criticize or judge yourself. Instead, simply acknowledge it as a Dis-EmPower thought. Then, add this quick and easy tool in the middle. Tell your mind, "Control - Pause - Delete." Just think of the Dis-EmPower thought coming in. You control that thought right at the edge of your mind (think of it as the boundary of your castle). You pause to determine that this is indeed a Dis-EmPower thought, then you delete it from your mind (basically kick it out of coming anywhere near your castle again).

Now for the crucial part, replace it quickly with a EmPower thought. Example: You can change "He was rude to me." to "I did not appreciate the choice of words he used." Instead of having something *done* to you. You've flipped the script. The power stays with you. Now release that thought. There is no point in trying to continue focusing on the Dis-EmPower thoughts. Transform it to a EmPower Thought and let it go. An easy way to remember this is a device I came up with: Control - Pause - Delete.

**Control** - Be observant of thought
**Pause** - Take a few deep breaths in and out. Instead of reacting instinctively, take a pause in the moment and transform the thought into a EmPower Thought
**Delete** - Release the thought

If this can get you to stop reacting on impulse and reacting to situations or other people, then you are halfway there.

For my extra credit chaos busters, if you really want to take this one step further, you can focus on inviting *three* EmPower in after you release your Dis-EmPower thought.

We want to wake up and be more conscious about life. You want to live your life by design instead of by default. Dis-EmPower thoughts will keep you in default mode. Your internal operating system will simply run on the easiest setting unless you take the time to customize it to your design. You see? You have the power! Everything really is in your control. You just have to pay attention to your expectations and thoughts and be open to transformation.

# CHAPTER 3 TOOLKIT

- Mindset is the ability to choose how you set your mind amidst the chaos. Mindset is a choice and a skill.
- When it comes to ugly tsunami chaos, once you start going downwards in the tornado of chaos spiral, you have to *consciously* realize what is happening in order for you to move back upwards.
- Chaos Tool 1: The Step Ladder - When you're so far down the downward spiral, your number one goal is to first become aware of your current state without judgement, blame, ridicule, or criticism of yourself or others. The second goal is simply to try get your state one step further up in your emotional ladder.

  o Gratitude 100 List - make a list of things you are grateful for
  o Shining a Light for Others - acts of kindness toward others can help you move up the step ladder.

- Chaos Tool 2: Ripples of Grief - Grieving anything is okay. Move at any speed you wish, but keep moving. Remember, they are ripples of grief for a reason. Ripples are not stationary.
- Chaos Tool 3: Chaos of Thoughts – Dis-Empower thoughts make you feel bad, crummy, or negative. EmPower thoughts are all about keeping your power within you and changing your perspective to create an empowering story.
- Use Control - Pause - Delete to let go of Dis-Empower thoughts

  o Control - Be observant of thought
  o Pause - Take a few deep breaths in and out. Pause.
  o Delete - Release the original thought and transform the thought into a EmPower thought

## Chapter 4

# PREVENTING TSUNAMI CHAOS IN THE MIND

**Everything starts in the mind. That's where it all starts. Knowing what you want is the first step toward getting it**
**- Mae West**

Now chaos busters, you have three tangible tools (and a few bonus tools) to use when you're caught in the middle of your tsunami chaos in the mind. But that is not enough! *How can I not even invite it in?* I'm sure you want to know how to *prevent* Tsunami Chaos, right? Alright, I hear you. I got you. Let's get started, shall we? I know you're dying to learn not on, not two, but many ways to keep that nasty tsunami chaos out of your beautiful ocean of life, right?

Well, fear no more chaos busters!

## CHAOS TOOL 1: SETTING YOUR INTENTION

I hate to tell you this, but none of these tools will work if you don't set an intention. You have to set your intention to change, make a difference in your ocean of life, and be willing to allow yourself to be open to new unchartered waters. Repeat after me: *I set my intention to welcome change. I am open to new and creative solutions that help me heal and grow. I set my intention to accept the new, and release the old.*

Cue in any other intentions that help you to remember why you're doing the inner work and why you need to keep going, especially when the waters get choppy.

I know you set an intention when you started reading this book. So you're already on the path of transformation. But what happens when you set out on uncharted waters and your co-captain (partner, spouse) or your crew on the ship (friends, family, society, culture) are skeptical or downright don't believe in what you're doing, and in essence don't believe in *you*?

You can't say "everything is going to be okay. I know what I'm doing." Because, well…you don't.

Especially when it comes to the unknown. Especially when it comes to alternative, natural, holistic approaches to your well-being and mental state. Especially when you're going to try something that is not the status quo. This goes for things like conventional medicine as well. The difference is that in conventional medicine, you put all your trust and faith in the hands of people you believe spent years of their life learning how to manage illnesses and disease and have credentials to do so. They must know what they're talking about, right? I know you're thinking that they know what *your unique body, mind,* and *spirit* needs, right?

Well, sorry to bust your bubble my friends, but not so much. They are equally as much risk, if not multiple times more. Conventional medicine should not be for treating anything other than an immediate life-death situation or dire medical intervention. Just think about it. You go to a conventional doctor with a headache. He prescribes you with a prescription drug of some sort, most likely without trying to figure out what is causing your headaches, or where the root of your issue is to begin with. You look at the side effects of this drug and realize it's worse than your headaches, in fact, much worse. You start taking the drug anyway because you trust your doctor only for it to lead to one of the side effects. Let's say ulcers. You go back to your doctor and now you're put on another drug for ulcers which has a side effect of heart issues. You see this vicious cycle that happens more often than you may think?

Well, I sure was not going to put my life in the hands of this system if I could help it. When I decided I had enough with the doctors treating me like a medical mystery on the brink of a carnival of surgeries, I set my intention. *I am going to find ways to heal myself naturally. I am not getting the surgery in six weeks. I will heal myself. Answers will come to me.*

Holistic, natural remedies were the only treatment I pursued and I had faith that as I searched, the answers would come. My family was stunned. My friends thought I was crazy. Everyone had good intentions. They all wanted what was best for me. But they couldn't even fathom how and why I would go against "expert medical advice." Who was I to challenge a physician who had years of practice? Who was I to say "no" to someone who told me I had a finite time to live and think that I was going to heal myself?

This is not easy by any means. Sometimes, it means to check in with your ego. Sometimes this means pushing through in unchartered waters alone. And, that's scary. You may even need to navigate through tough crowds that maybe even your family or loved ones have joined in with.

But, guess what? You need to push through, not because you are determined and persistent. Not because you are stubborn and will push through anything. Not because you want to go against the odds to be different.

It's because it is the *right* thing to do! And, doing the right thing no matter how hard it is will never fail you. You will always have your principles, your purpose, your dignity, your value, and your sense of peace.

Let me tell you, even my own husband couldn't understand why I would take such a chance. I had no medical background. I had three young children and a whole life ahead of me to live. Couldn't I just get the surgeries and hope for the best? Well, yes, I could. But was that my only choice? Absolutely not. Once I set my intention that there clearly had to be another way, I was resolved. I knew I was going to find that way no matter what. It was scary but it was also liberating. I knew in my heart of hearts that this would work out. It had to. I *had* to because it was the right thing to do. I owed it to myself and my family to find another way, find a *better* way to heal and transform myself. What I did not realize at the time, is that by healing and transforming myself, I am taking my family on this journey as well to heal and transform themselves.

All it takes is one person in a relationship to transform the relationship and the others involved in that relationship.

And so it worked. Shortly after I set my intention, answers started coming to me. I'm serious! I would be looking at my Facebook feed and all of the sudden an advertisement would pop up on the side about reiki or Ayurveda. Or I'd scroll through my e-mail and receive a newsletter about a healing modality I had not considered. It kept happening. People would "randomly" mention something their family member had gone through and how that person healed naturally. The universe was sending me exactly what I needed. There was no better proof than that to support my intention.

To set your intention, think about what you want to happen. What is your *why?* Really focus on that, your *why.* And declare it. Write it down. Feel it. Breathe your intention in and out. And feel the feelings you would feel once you achieved your intention right now in the moment. Don't wait until after you actually achieved it. Even though I was in immense pain, I visualized how I would feel once I was healthy and strong. I invited those feelings in the present moment, even if it was only a few minutes at a time. Those few minutes helped me remember my *why* and *how* I want to feel.

They key is to vibrate in that feeling of how you want to feel as if that's already how you feel right now in the moment. I liked to call it "Presentizing" the future. I visualized myself on the beach looking and feeling great and really used all my five senses to feel the wind in my hair, smell the salty ocean water, feel the warm sand under my feet, and hear the seagulls soaring high. I let my imagination run wild and for those few minutes of visualizing, I felt amazing.

# CHAOS TOOL 2: ENHANCING YOUR INTUITION

Once you've set your intention, you have to enhance and trust in your own natural intuition. Everyone has it - it is no magic pill that only those with a crystal ball have. My friends, you were born with intuition. In fact, you even used it when you were a baby. Have you seen how babies and young kids naturally gravitate toward some people and yet shy away from others? They are picking up on the complementary vibrations. They're drawn to "good" energy.

But as kids get older, they are forced to go toward people or even do things that they instinctively know not to do, but do it anyway due to pressure from parents, family, siblings, friends, and society in general. Can you think of a time you did something because someone told you to do it? How did you feel? Was there a small part of you that knew this wasn't for you? That's intuition. But all too often we naturally learn to put our intuition aside and listen to the exterior world. We shut out our intuition and listen to others instead, for better, or for worse.

Now, it is time you start bringing that intuition back into your conscious mind and actually start listening to it. This takes time. It isn't easy. Especially when you're conditioned to second guess your intuition in the face of advice from others. But just like every other muscle or skill, it can be learned. The more you use it, the better you'll get at it. I suggest you start small. Use the five second rule game.

Ask yourself a question and see what answer crops up in less than five seconds. Don't think too much or use your brain to contemplate. Just count down from five and take the first answer that comes into your mind. Keep practicing this little by little. I promise, with due practice, you will gain trust in your own intuition.

For example, let's say you have two job offers and you can't decide which one to choose. Close your eyes, and take a couple deep breaths in and out. Then ask yourself should I take Job A or Job B and see what immediately comes to you. Don't overthink it or try to put an answer in your brain. You'll be surprised that you even get an answer at first.

The more you practice, the faster the answers will come. Sometimes, even before you finish a question.

I'm telling you it is so important. You must gain trust in your intuition. This way you will build faith around your decision, or whatever you decide to do for your wellness. Only then will you be able to push through any of the challenges that may come your way and address anyone from your support system if they do not agree with your choice.

Sometimes, the answer will surprise your conscious mind. Maybe it won't even make sense. But it's in your subconscious mind where ninety percent the "work" happens, and the answers will always make sense to your subconscious mind.

Another intuition skill builder I like to use is called the Pendulum Approach. I liked this exercise when I first started experimenting with my intuition. I doubted myself a lot for feeling a certain way based on what the doctors were telling me. I even doubted myself because of my friends and family. Everyone told me I was crazy and foolish for "ignoring sound medical advice." I had to rely upon my own strength and inner wisdom. And believe me, I didn't really trust it. So, I needed something else, something more tangible that I could visibly see. I needed another mechanism that would validate what my own intuition was telling me. That's how I started using the Pendulum Approach. It works like this.

First, grab a necklace with a medium weighted pendant hanging from it. You don't want anything too heavy, but you also don't want anything that is too light. The necklace should be able to swing back and forth when you hold it from the top. The weight of the pendant hangs on the bottom.

Once you have your necklace, sit down and hold the necklace shoulder height and about a foot from your body. Ask an easy "yes" or "no" question, where the answer is yes, such as "Is today Saturday?" or "Is my name (your name)?" Observe what direction the pendulum starts to swing. Typically, it will go sideways (left to right or right to left) or front to back.

Whatever direction the pendulum goes is now your "yes" answer direction.

Hang with me here, you're doing great!

Now, ask another question that you know the answer is "no." For example, "Is this the year 3000?" See which way the pendulum swings. It should go in the opposite direction as your "yes" answer. If "Yes" was side to side, then "no" would be front to back. With your directions set, you can ask the burning question you grabbed the pendulum for in the first place. Use a simple sentence with a clear yes or no answer. Do not ask open ended questions such as "what should I do about this?"

If the pendulum spins in circles or doesn't move at all, please don't give up. Try asking the question in a different way or simply put the necklace down and come back to it later in the day. Work on the pendulum method often and keep practicing to build up your trust in your own intuition. By setting an intention and enhancing your intuition, you will start to feel yourself slowly preventing tsunami chaos. It really works!

# CHAOS TOOL 3: THE MYTH OF TIME

When it comes to preventing tsunami chaos in the mind, time can be a huge villain in our valiant attempts to thwart the chaos. People often ask me where I find the time to do everything that I do. I find the question an interesting one. It is as if I have a magic treasure chest in my closet that no one knows about and I secretly find more hours in the day than anyone else. False. We know that isn't true. It is impossible. What I do know is that we often think that there is no time to do everything we want to do. "I'm busy" are three words that are uttered so often in our everyday conversations.

Don't you wish you had more time to do the things you love? Spoiler alert – *You do!* We often think there is no time to do everything we want to do, yet we allow ourselves to spend time on things (most times unknowingly) that really are not in alignment with our purpose. As I started digging deeper and looking into my day in a schedule format, I became aware of how I was spending my time on who, on what, where, doing what. Take it a step further, I learned how I felt doing those things. I also figured out if I was the *only* person who could do those things. Could someone else do them? It was clear to me that I can really find time to **have** everything I want. But that doesn't necessarily mean I need to **do** everything I want. Stay with me.

Imagine you're starting a business. You love to make designs and graphics to promote the business and you're amazing at it. You have great ideas and a vision usually, but you really struggle with creating business plans or dealing with numbers. When you have to work with a spreadsheet and crunch out numbers, it takes you hours to put together. Then you get mad because you don't have time to work on the elements of the business that you love, the things you are good at.

Is there anyone you could bring in as a partner to handle the analytics/business plan side of things? Do you have someone you trust? Letting someone who excels in that realm can provide a win-win-win. You win because you get to spend your time on your strengths. Your partner wins because they're contributions are valued. You both win, as does your business, because your combined superpowers and genius zones (things you excel at and love doing) are contributing to the success of the business.

Make a list of the things you love to do, the things you are good at, the things you hate to do, and the things you struggle with. See a correlation? Now you can tap into that treasure chest of time by finding resources to help you with the "don't do well/hate" tasks, or what I affectionately call the "I suck at these" tasks. Another exercise I practice is the Timeclock. Try this.

Visualize your day in a 24-hour timeclock. All of us have 24 hours in our day. To become aware of how you're currently spending your time, I want you to map out those 24 hours. What do you do in each one? How do you feel? What people/places/things are associated with each action? Are you the only person who can do that activity?

This is an exercise on awareness. Most of us aren't aware of how we "waste" time. When we feel we don't have enough time to accomplish everything we want to, ugly chaos starts brewing.

By mapping out your timeclock of a day, you get to see exactly how you're spending each hour. Really analyze it. For those tasks that are taking too long or that you don't enjoy, can anyone in your life help you with them? If so, delegate. It may be hard, especially if you're a Type A perfectionist like me. But wouldn't you rather spend your time blocks doing the things you are good at and enjoy? I know I do!

Don't get me wrong here. Delegate does not necessarily mean you have to pay someone to do it. I know your mind is racing with all kinds of excuses about how you can't afford to pay someone, etc. Remember, when you seek the answers will come. Enlist your kids into things. Maybe there's a high school kid down the block that's looking for some experience in an area that you need help in. Maybe you have a stay-at-home mom that's looking to go back in to work but wants more experience. There are plenty of "resources" out there and options if only you keep an open mind, an abundance mindset, and just ask!

Before going to bed, take a look at your timeclock worksheet. Really look at it and conceptualize your time. Practice doing this for a week and see if you can discover anything new about how you spend your precious 24 hours. Now, write down what you plan to do the next day and how you want to feel doing those activities or tasks. For example, "wake up at 0700 feeling refreshed, rejuvenated, and rested." The more you can get congruent with planning out your next day and how you want to feel, the more you'll start feeling positive when that moment comes, and the more positive you feel, the more positive things you will attract. See what an amazing cycle this can be?

The myth of time is just that. I mean, time was created by man to categorize moments in the day. It is a construct. You can't touch it. You can't smell it. You can't even really feel it (though I admit you can feel time passing in your body). Why is it so scary? Time may be this precious resource that isn't infinite, but it is malleable and can be used to help you live your best life, by design. Time isn't limiting. You are not "too busy." Stop saying you are "busy." Start figuring out how you spend your time and who/what/where you spend your time on. Start living for you. You must live for yourself first and grow yourself, before you can help or serve others.

Chaos busters, if you practice these exercises, you will be primed to prevent the ugly chaos in the mind. By now you have tools on how to manage and prevent that ugly tsunami chaos in the mind. In our next chapter, we'll take a deep dive into tsunami chaos in the body.

Stay tuned for how to look at the concept of energy when it comes to "time management" as well! You'd be surprised, is it really a question of time management, or is it really all about energy management? Thank you for sticking with it. Thank you for being ALL IN.

## CHAPTER 4 TOOLKIT

- Chaos Tool 1: Set your intention with conviction
- Chaos Tool 2: Enhancing your intuition - bring that intuition back into your conscious mind and actually start listening to it.
- Chaos Tool 3: The myth of time - We often think that there is no time to do everything we want to do, yet we allow ourselves to spend time on things (most times unknowingly) that really are not in alignment with our purpose.

  - Visualize your day in a 24-hour timeclock. All of us have 24 hours in our day. Map out those 24 hours. What do you do in each one?

*Chapter 5*

# PREVENTING TSUNAMI CHAOS IN THE BODY

**By understanding how our body really works-- meaning what it is meant to do and how it is meant to do it, we can also understand what it is not meant to do.**
-Jothi Dugar

Okay, Chaos busters. Now you have a few tools in your arsenal to prevent that ugly chaos in your mind. You can recognize it. You can handle it. And now, you can prevent it. The mind is the place to start. But what do we do about that ugly chaos in the body?

We store emotions, trauma, stress, and unprocessed feelings in our bodies. Remember that thought or feeling that was frustrating you about someone or something? You pushed that thought away. Well, guess what? If you didn't actually take a moment to process it, learn from it, and release it, it's still within you, it will stay in your cells, your tissues, and even your organs. That storage can cause a world of trouble. In fact, these things may even present themselves as physical symptoms or "dis-ease."

Have you ever wondered why someone that has had a lot of "heartaches" when it comes to love and relationships "suddenly" has a heart attack? Or take someone that has developed a "weird" pain in the stomach (otherwise called Solar Plexus chakra) right when they are in the middle of a career crisis that really never went away and now has turned into chronic pain that's undiagnosed? Yes, chaos can make you feel sick. But rather than run to the drug store to find the first medicinal band-aid you see, let's try something different.

Let's get to the root of that trouble, the root of that pain. The sooner we realize the mind-body energy connection, the sooner we can take action. If we're able to resolve things and release them at our thoughts-feelings-emotions level, then we don't need to wait for them to manifest into our physical bodies at all.

You guys, after that traumatic c-section, my body went into a whole state of ugly chaos. Yes, it was in part due to the burnout and negligence of that doctor, but it also was a bit of a transformation point for me. When I say I spent months in excruciating pain, I'm talking about the kind of pain that it hurt to breathe. It hurt to live. But I knew in my heart that I was going to live.

**I wanted to live, and that was enough.**

No amount of pain killers were going to take away my physical pain. In fact, all they would do is mask that pain. I had to feel it. I had to feel the pain of being an overachiever with ridiculously high expectations for myself. I had to feel the pain of trying to be the perfect wife, the perfect mother, the perfect employee, the perfect friend. I had to feel the pain of letting myself down when I couldn't be those perfect things because of the physical pain I was in.

If it wasn't for that pain, I wouldn't have opened my mind and heart to alternative healing modalities. I wouldn't have even given myself the chance and felt worthy of healing myself from the inside out, not just my body, but my mind, and my soul. I wouldn't have learned all these lessons I'm able to share with you today. I had to go on this journey to become The Chaos Guru.

My pain had a purpose. Every pain has a purpose. It tells us things. It sends signals to our brain that something isn't right. The faster we act on it, the faster we can move to the next level of our very existence. By understanding how our body really works-- meaning what it is meant to do and how it is meant to do it, we can also understand what it is NOT meant to do. The way our body works is quite simple, yet we all try to complicate simple things as humans because we just cannot allow ourselves to believe in the basic and simple principles of life. You don't have to go through a life threatening emotional, mental, or physical traumatic event to figure it out.

It all starts with a little awareness, or should I say consciousness. You need a base point, really. Think of a time when you felt totally at ease. Remember those calm, placid waters from the beginning of our journey? What was going on in your life during that peaceful time? How did your body feel? I bet you felt healthy, happy, and relaxed, just to name a few. Now, think of a situation when you felt an abundance of stress or chaos in your life. Goodness, it could be right now! Instead of focusing on those stressful triggers (your workload, relationship disagreements, financial concerns, etc.) purely in your mind, I want you to do a check-in with your body.

Where did you feel that tension?
Was it in your shoulders?
Your back?
Your stomach?
How did you feel physically?
Were you fatigued?
Under the weather?
In any sort of pain?
What did you feel in that part of your body?
Was it warm?
Did it feel tight?
Was it sharp or dull?
Heavy or light?
Don't worry, there is no right or wrong answer here.

By comparing your body in these two states: the state of calm and the state of ugly chaos, you can see a huge difference. In fact, you can *feel* a huge difference. Now, the "old" you would have either plowed through the chaos and ignored the warning signs your body was so graciously giving you. Or perhaps you would have increased your caffeine intake, or T.V. time, or maybe even chose to focus on your work more if the chaos originated from family. Whatever you *used* to do, it doesn't matter. There are no judgements here, and please let go of any judgements you are placing on yourself.

You are here today reading this book and that's already a step in the right direction. Congratulate yourself for that achievement as 99% of that world is behind you already. What matters is the here and the now. Well, what are you waiting for? Do you want to learn the tools that you can use to prevent ugly chaos in the body? Let's jump right in!

# CHAOS TOOL 1: MINDFUL MOVING

How many of you wake up, check your phone for e-mails, crawl out of bed, go to the bathroom, brush your teeth, and start the rest of your morning routine as if you're on autopilot? So often, we hit the "cruise control" button on our lives. Which is why it becomes easy to disregard pain and warning signals that something is amiss. We just keep going and going and going. I need you to tap those brakes.

Mindful moving is just that, taking time to consciously and mindfully move throughout the day. It doesn't have to be a hardcore exercise routine, or a one-hour meditation walk through the park. I'm talking five minutes. Get up every hour for five minutes and move. As you move, notice your movement. Feel the texture of the ground below you. What can you see? What do you hear? Take a little walk around your office, your home, your block, your neighborhood. Whatever you have the time and space to try. Keep the earphones out of your ears. Keep that phone in your pocket (or leave it on your desk if you can).

Focus on the five senses in great detail. It's okay to have thoughts. When they come, just acknowledge them as a passing stranger, and see them disappear. Talk to your mind instead of letting it talk to you and tell your mind to focus on your senses and observe your surroundings. This is not a "thinking" exercise. It's a "doing" and "being" exercise.

If you're outside, focus on one sense at a time and observe what you feel, see, hear, or even taste. If you're inside, do the same as you walk around your room, office, or whatever location you're in. Your senses are very powerful. Combined, they have the ability to ground you. Existing in the present moment will help you find the calm your body and your mind is craving. It will also help to rewire your brain and calm your parasympathetic nervous system.

To help you refine some of your techniques even more, try these little brain hacking tricks. As you mindfully walk, rub your pointer finger and your thumb together gently. Feel the sensation between your fingers. Feel the warmth that little touch of friction creates. Just allow yourself to focus on that feeling for 30 seconds. Once you've become comfortable, you can try this with other daily tasks in your life. Rather than unconsciously brushing your teeth, feel the bristles tickle your gums. What does your toothpaste smell like? What does it taste like?

Use the five senses in every activity that you can. Build your foundation of mindful movement with each practice. Even if it feels silly at first, stay with it. You will find that it is a quick and easy way to ground in the present moment and take a break from living on autopilot. Best of all the more you allow yourself to do these simple, yet massively effective techniques throughout the day, and incorporate them into the activities you are already doing, the faster you will start seeing a positive difference in your attitude, your happiness, performance, effectiveness, and your energy.

# CHAOS TOOL 2: SHAKE IT OFF

When Ugly Chaos mounts in the body, it can be all too easy to enter flight or fight mode. Now, we all know that the precious "fight or flight," is an evolutionary trait to keep us safe. It is a mechanism built into our species to protect us from harm. Unfortunately, this response is very sensitive. Gone are the days when we only triggered the flight or fight response in the wake of physical danger. We do this for emotional triggers too.

Stress invites a buildup of cortisol in our systems thanks to that nifty flight or fight thing. Too much cortisol can cause our whole body to get out of whack. High levels can cause agitation, sugar cravings, increased belly fat, and other physical ailments. Low levels of cortisol can cause fatigue and unstable moods.

So how do we combat this? In the words of singer Taylor Swift, we can "shake, shake, shake it off." Stay with me here. The physical act of shaking our bodies releases endorphins. Endorphins are awesome. Shaking is a natural response to extreme stress. Have you ever seen dogs do a body shake to calm themselves down? Sometimes they do it before or after transitioning to a new activity like coming in from a walk or after playing. Even athletes shake themselves off before a major race or game.

To shake it off, you don't need a lot of time or energy. Just set aside a few minutes to yourself if you can. First, before you get into the heart of the movement, pause. Take a couple deep and long breaths in and out to allow yourself to use your breath to get into a calm state. Start by shaking your hands, watch your fingers dangle. Gradually shake your arms and shoulders. From there, you can move to the hips and legs. Finally, and this is the last part, shake your head. Just let go until you feel loose. If you can, you can even put on some upbeat music to really get into it. Maybe cue some Taylor Swift! (I am kidding). The movement gives your body an outlet to release the stress and tension that built up during the flight or fight response. While you can't see it, you are releasing that energy into the world and cleansing your body as you do it. Plus, it is fun, and you can do it just about anywhere.

My third and final tool for releasing ugly chaos in the body may take a few tries before you really get it. But I believe in you!

# CHAOS TOOL 3: MOTION
# AFFECTS YOUR E-MOTION

We've talked about how everything is related - mind, body, and energy. I hope by now you're starting to see connections across these three sectors. Now it is time to learn how changing your physiology affects your e-motion.

Mindful movement grounds you and helps you focus on a present moment. Shaking it off releases endorphins to combat stress. Movement can free negative emotions.

When you feel positive emotions, there is no reason to change. But when you're feeling like you're in that downward spiral of emotions, the fastest way to work back up the tornado of chaos to those positive emotions is to change physicality. That translates to "get up and move." Yes, change your physical space. If you can't leave your physical space, change your physical direction. On a call with a client? If your environment permits, put them on speaker phone and face another direction with your body. Try some squats. Stand on your tiptoes. Do *anything* that puts your body in a totally different space. If you're bending down or crunching your body when you're on the phone, hold your head up high and straighten your spine. If you're feeling anxious, pace around in a circle. Tapping your leg as you sit? Stand up for a few moments and maybe turn around a few times (slowly).

I have had moments where I felt blocked creatively and then I simply changed directions physically, and the block released. My e-motion changed! I encourage you to try this and notice how you feel.

Another tool you can try, that is related to this one, is the smile method. I love this one. I use it often. Put a smile on your face, no matter the situation.

"Right Jothi, I'll look like a maniac."

Maybe. Maybe not. Even if you are in a heated argument, smile.

(This is way easier to do on the phone). It is impossible for you to smile with your whole face and remain angry and frustrated with someone. Sure it may feel forced at first, but give it a few tries. Trust me, it works.

Have a difficult conversation coming up? Practice it and smile a few times before you start your conversation. Smiling is contagious. (But so is getting hijacked by your "sabatogers").

Smiling brings out your own sage and attracts others' sage potential as well. At least try it. I know you will notice a difference.

You got this!

## CHAPTER 5 TOOLKIT

- We store emotions, trauma, stress, and unprocessed feelings in our bodies.
- Chaos Tool 1: Mindful Moving - take time to consciously and mindfully move throughout the day
- Chaos Tool 2: Shake It Off - the physical act of shaking our bodies releases endorphins
- Chaos Tool 3: Motion Affects Your E-motion - Movement can free negative emotions by changing your physicality.

*Chapter 6*

# PREVENTING TSUNAMI CHAOS IN THE ENERGY

"The higher your energy level, the more efficient your body. The more efficient your body, the better you feel and the more you will use your talent to produce outstanding results."
-Tony Robbins

Welcome back my friends. If you are feeling a little overwhelmed with all this talk about tsunami chaos, I want you to know that is perfectly okay. It can be overwhelming. It is a lot to process. I know. I've been there. We've talked about what to do when ugly chaos manifests in our minds. I've given you some great tools to combat ugly chaos in the body. Now it is time we take a look at the third part of the connection: energy.

It's a tough one to wrap our heads around. And it is not as "woo woo" as you may think. In living creatures, this energy is otherwise known as our life force energy, qui, prana, etc. And, like most things, if we don't understand how our energy works and how it is connected to our mind and body, we can be inadvertently adding more chaos to our lives and to others. When you are in a "bad mood", you are giving off "bad vibes" or in essence projecting an energy of negativity onto yourself and others in your surrounding. Other people pick up on those vibes instantly. They can sense that something is off with your energy. Others will, to some degree, *absorb* some of your negative energy. Even if you didn't mean it, it still happens.

Ok, Jothi, well how can I control something I don't even know is happening?

I got you.

I know you may be sick of hearing this, but yes, it comes down to awareness! Learning how your energy affects yourself and others is the best thing you can do. You have to learn how to treat your energy.

Let's take a look at our first tool.

# CHAOS TOOL 1: TREAT YOUR ENERGY LIKE MONEY

When you were a little kid, did you earn an allowance? If not, I'm sure you can remember your first job. Was there ever something you really wanted to buy and saved your money for? You saved and saved until you could finally buy that ultimate purchase. When you finally did buy whatever you had your heart set on, it felt really good, didn't it?

As adults, we use money for all sorts of things. Pay bills, buy gifts, treat ourselves to things, care for those we love, invest in our passions, you get the picture. The older and wiser we get, the more valuable money becomes. We get a little choosier when it comes to how we spend our money.

Chaos busters, I want you to treat your energy like money. When we recognize the value of our energy, we'll learn to respect it. Imagine you get in a disagreement with your colleague. That tiff sets you off all day. You're so upset with this individual that you are completely blind to the positive things that are happening around you. Your bad mood or "negative vibes" are being absorbed by those around you. By the end of the day, you're exhausted. You're grumpy. You get in a fight with your spouse. You don't even know where the day went because you were so fixated on the disagreement you had with that individual. That my friends, is a telltale example of expending your energy unwisely.

Another way to look at it is this. Imagine when you wake up in the morning, you have 25 marbles. For every task you do throughout the day, you have to give up a marble. Some tasks take more marbles than others. You don't want to end the day with zero marbles. But there is a catch, there are activities and tasks that actually *give* you more marbles. These are positive, renewing, self-care tasks that refresh your spirit. So as you go through your day, are you going to focus on the things that take away your marbles? Or are you going to channel your energy into things that give you marbles? The choice is yours.

Manage your energy well. Spend it wisely. Don't waste it on negativity. Or, you'll end up with zero marbles at the end of the day. When people ask me how I have the "time" to do everything I am doing, my response is always that I have the same amount of time as everyone, but I choose to manage my energy well. That's where the money is folks. Where focus goes, energy flows, and results show. That is the famous mantra, right? So, focus on your end goals, your dreams, and what fills you up, and your energy will naturally flow there fueling your body and giving you the push you need to take on anything.

My next tool for you is another tactic you can practice anytime, anywhere. It is called EFT Tapping. EFT stands for Emotional Freedom Technique. It is a technique that combines the ancient concept through the Chinese system of meridian lines. The Chinese believe there are millions of meridian lines running throughout your body and there are several points where these meridian points connect. Instead of using needles or intense pressure, you can release blocks in your energetic system by tapping. How cool is that?

EFT also marries that technique with pseudo psychology -- combining tapping with affirmations and statements on the negative side and positive side. This takes your brain from what it might currently be feeling, acknowledges that, and allows you to shift to a positive feeling. The more often you do it, the easier it will become. EFT can also be used to release negative emotions you may have been suppressing or have not processed yet.

# CHAOS TOOL 2: INTRO TO EFT TAPPING

Okay, to get started, take three deep breaths and let them out very slowly. I'll wait. Next, rate how you are feeling on a scale from one to ten with ten being the worst. Now it is time to start tapping.

There are several tapping points throughout the body. You can watch a video on tapping on my website www.jothidugar.com/resources. To start, you can find the first tapping point at the crown of your head, right in the middle between the back of your head and the front. You can start by spreading out your fingers and gently tapping around that area for about five seconds.

The next tapping point is right on the inside of the eyebrow, close to the bridge of your nose. You can choose which eyebrow to tap and use two fingers or one, whichever feels more comfortable. Now move to the outer side of your eye. You can feel that bone along your temple, and that is where you want to tap. Remember, friends, only five or so seconds and be very gentle! You don't have to count the number of taps or add a specific rhythm to it.

The next point is underneath the eye, below the eye socket. This is the place where if you have bad sinuses, you can usually feel pressure. Then move to below your nose. You will want to tap that soft spot between the top of your lip and the base of your nose, right in the middle. After this spot you can move to the middle of your chin. Now it is time to move to your collarbone area. You can tap on one or both. Play around with it! The next tapping spot is under the armpit, about a quarter of the way down your side.

The last part is the finger points. I truly believe finger points make a huge difference thanks to the millions of nerves that are stored there. All you have to do is take one finger and tap the outer edge of each finger of the opposite hand.

You can do EFT tapping on either side of your body. You can switch. You can do it anyway that feels good to you. Once you complete that rotation from the top to the fingers, take another deep breath in and out a couple times and see how you feel. Rate the pain/emotion/feeling in your body on a scale from 1-20 with one being feeling great, and 10 being you feel totally out of control. If the number went down from how you felt before tapping, but not yet down to a 2 or 3, that just means you have to keep going. Try to repeat the cycle a few more times and rate yourself each time. This usually takes about 10-15 minutes.

Even a quick tapping of two to five minutes should do the trick if you're caught in the moment.

The other tapping point that is commonly used is the karate chop point. If you were to attempt a karate chop, this is the point on the outer edge of your hand that would make contact with whatever you were chopping. It is about an inch or two below the pinky. If you're in a public place or at work and you wanted a quick way to release some blocks you are facing, you can do this instead of the other points. Just the act of this will get you back into that neutral balance and calm state, even if you don't use affirmations alongside the practice. It is a great way to quickly try to rebalance in the moment.

Once you've become more comfortable with this practice, you can introduce some pseudo psychology into the mix. Say these affirmations out loud or quietly as you tap:

- Even though my mind is buzzing with the number of things I have to do right now, I want to find clarity and calm bit by bit.
- Even though this mental pressure to solve the problem is stressing me out, I'm open to allowing myself to slow down so I can think more clearly.
- Even though I feel so overwhelmed right now, I know I am doing my best and I can do so much more when I am relaxed.

When you complete the exercise, take a deep breath and let it out. Rate yourself again from one to ten and see how your energy has shifted from the start of the practice to its conclusion. If you don't reach a rating of four or below just yet, repeat the whole exercise a few times more and see where you get.

EFT can be therapeutic and very comprehensive to heal deep wounds, so this is just a small taste of it. You can also use EFT just to let things out and vent. When you feel angry, frustrated, or have some pent-up emotions, instead of suppressing them inside, or letting them out onto others, just go to a quiet place and air it all out. Let it all go. Say whatever you want to say while tapping on your EFT points. You'll notice that as you do that, what's really bothering you inside may come to light. Your subconscious blocks or fears may come to the surface for you to take a moment to become aware of. And, awareness is half the battle! Once you become aware of them, you can start to truly heal the roots of your pain, trauma, triggers, and chaos.

EFT is a deeply healing technique and if you have trauma that goes back several years or even to your childhood or earlier, you may need to seek a professional EFT Specialist or Practitioner. Don't worry, I am also a certified EFT practitioner and factor in EFT exercises into my transformational programs. I hope by now you know how to reach me and have built up some trust in me! Just in case you forgot, here is my website: www.jothidugar.com.

## CHAOS TOOL 3: PEACE BEGINS WITH ME

This is a tool that is easy to do and brings peace within your mind. It is really simple and amazing. All you're going to do is tap your index finger to your thumb. Then tap your middle finger to your thumb. Follow that with your ring finger and then finally your pinky. You're just going to tap each one in a rhythmic fashion. You don't have to go too fast or too slow, whatever feels right for you.

Next, try to get your mind away from the other things you are facing in the day and bring your awareness back to the sensation you are feeling in your fingers. Allow yourself to focus just on the sensation of touch in your fingertips. If you find yourself wanting to look around during this exercise, close your eyes if you can. The next step is to add the affirmation. It is, "Peace begins with me."

If you are in a place where you can say it out loud, say each word as you tap each finger to your thumb. "Peace" would be your index finger. "Begins" would be your middle finger, and so on. Obviously, if you can't say the affirmation out loud you can recite it in your head.

This is another way to focus on bringing your awareness to the mantra and the sensation in your hand. The more you practice this, the better you will be able to get your mind off of the chaos and focus on one single thing in the moment. Peace Begins with Me is also a great way to rewire your brain. Friends, you know by now that calm begins within you. Love begins with you. Serenity begins within you. You can switch up the words to ones that really resonate with you.

By just tapping on your fingers you will quickly shift your brain from focusing on the negative to the positive. Repeat this for at least a minute until you feel a sense of peace in your mind. See? It really is *that* easy! Mindfulness and these simple little in-the-moment techniques can really help you calm the chaotic waters of tsunami chaos in your energy. Bank that energy. Store it up for the things you enjoy in life. Don't waste energy on negative emotions, feeling angry or resentful about others or your situation, snowball stress, or anything that can add physical and emotional turmoil in your life.

Yes, I know, it is impossible to be happy and positive all of the time. I'm not asking you to do that. I'm just saying when you cultivate an awareness of the negative feelings and energy, you can quickly recognize it, allow yourself to feel it, process it, then release it. Then, invite in the gratefulness for everything you already have in your life in the moment and reinforce positive feelings and energy. That quick switch eliminates wasted time and well, wasted energy! To watch my video demonstrating this technique, visit www.jothidugar.com/resources.

## CHAPTER 6 TOOLKIT

- Tsunami chaos in the energy can be a tough concept to wrap your mind around, but it is not as "woo woo" as you may think.
- When you boil everything down to the smallest level, it boils down to a form of energy
- Chaos Tool 1: Treat Your Energy Like Money - manage your energy well and spend it wisely
- Chaos Tool 2: Intro to EFT Tapping - there are several tapping points throughout the body. A quick tapping of about two to five minutes can help you calm in the moment
- Chaos Tool 3: Peace Begins with Me - Simply by tapping each finger to your thumb and saying the words "Peace Begins with Me," you can calm the chaos in your energy.

*Chapter 7*

# RIP TIDE CHAOS (BAD CHAOS)

**Invisible forces of energy surround us at all times that may be adding to our bad chaos. When we become aware of them, we can transform them for our own good.**
**-Jothi Dugar**

Congratulations, my friends! We've made it through the tsunami chaos lessons. We're out! I hope you feel stronger and better equipped to handle that ugly chaos when it enters your life. I knew you could do it! Thank you for sticking with me.

I focused a lot on the tsunami chaos because I feel like that is what we face the most, as humans. There are plenty more tips and tools you can use. I invite you to schedule a Chaos Clarity Call with me on my website www.jothidugar.com so that I can customize tools to fit your exact situations! And now, let's dip our toes in the waters of rip tide chaos, or shall I say bad chaos for a moment. Don't worry, this is not going to be as intense as our tsunami chaos journey.

Bad chaos is the chaos that we're not always aware of. It is a sort of unknown chaos that is constantly affecting us without our knowledge. Remember, when you're standing in the ocean and a rip tide comes out of nowhere, catching you off guard? That is exactly what bad chaos does. But, like tsunami chaos, it can easily be released once you are aware of it.

That awareness starts with a holistic assessment of your personality, energy type, body type, special energy, and a variety of different factors. Yeah, a little bit of everything. By now, you trust me, right? This is not "woo woo." There is actually a science and physics behind all the "woo woo" anyway. Who knew that wearing the wrong clothes for your energy type could cause chaos in your life? Or if you're not doing the type of work that is compatible with your personality type, you're setting yourself up for a blah type of life?

You may have heard about the Myers-Briggs Type Indicator. It is a self-administered questionnaire that ultimately categorizes people into different "types" based on how they perceive the world around them and how they make decisions. The questions are simple and there are many free MBTI tests you can try on the internet. But the MBTI test will place you into one of 16 personality types. The types are all the possible combinations of the following eight identifiers: introvert, extrovert, intuition, sensing, thinking, feeling, perceiving, and judging.

The letters INTJ or ENFP are MBTI personality types. (introvert, intuition, thinking, judging) or (extrovert, intuition, feeling, perceiving). MBTI tests are fun because they also tend to be really accurate. You'll see a lot of your personality traits and quirks come to light after completing an assessment. Okay, so what does this have to do with bad chaos? Well friends, if these personality traits are true to you, then wouldn't it make sense that jobs, relationships, other life trajectories will either clash or harmonize with you based on these traits?

For example, let's look at someone who has an F in their personality type. The F stands for feeling. The thinking vs. feeling category is based on how you prefer to make decisions. A "feeler" is someone who relies on gut feelings, instinct, and tends to use their intuition to problem solve vs analytics or even logic. "Feelers" don't rely on following the order of operations when solving a problem. A "feeler" takes actions and builds relationships based on the gut feeling or intuition they have with that person, not based solely on their outward appearance or words. A "feeler" is someone who might buy a car just because it *feels* right sitting in it, and all other aspects like cost, fuel economics all come secondary.

On the contrary, "thinkers" are logical, analytical, and can be by the book. These people crave organizational structure and process when it comes to decision making. They show their work. They buy things based on the analytics and logistics behind the reasoning of buying something.

Now, imagine these two personality types in a work environment. If a boss requires his team to submit productivity reports at the beginning of each week, documenting all the work completed for the week prior, thinkers and feelers are going to approach the task differently. Feelers may wait until Sunday and dig through their e-mails to determine what tasks they completed for the report. Thinkers were completing the report throughout the week so it would be ready to go on Monday.

Awareness can be eye opening. We cause a lot of bad chaos when we're unaware of our personality triggers and those of others. We're literally wired to prefer to do things a certain way. MBTI helps bring to light what those ways are. Awareness and understanding allow us to articulate our personality traits to others to foster understanding and acceptance AND be aware of pitfalls we may have due to these traits. While each personality type has strengths and areas of weakness, all personality types are essential to the world around us! We need logical planners as much as we need passionate dreamers.

I highly recommend if you have the opportunity, to look at your work life. Is it conducive to your personality type? You might be doing the wrong type of work simply because your personality is pulling you elsewhere. You could be making plenty of money and supporting your family, but because this clash between your personality type and professional life causes chaos, you are bringing that bad chaos with you wherever you go. That means it comes home with you at the end of the day. It goes out to dinner with you. It goes to bed with you. You didn't even know it was there, right?

After you determine your MBTI, check online for a few free career aptitude tests based on MBTI types. It is a great starting point to see where you fit. It should come as no surprise that the things you're really fired up about happen to align with the career paths suggested for your MBTI type.

Just like we have different personality types, we also have different body types. Have you ever wondered why you look, think, feel, and act the way you do? I mean, why are you pre-dispositioned to certain habits and tendencies with food, sleep, and even illnesses? We each have a different body type. Sure, on the outside that is obvious. If we got in a line right now, we'd see major differences in our physiques. However, the differences go far beyond what can be seen by the naked eye. Your body type affects you from the food you eat to the exercise you do.

No, I'm not talking about weight management or going on a diet. I'm talking about fundamental cellular elements that are impacted by the choices you make each and every day.

"Jothi, you're not going to suggest a meal plan for me, are you?"

No, friends. I am not. But I am going to suggest you try an Ayervedic test.

"A WHAT?" you say.

Ayurveda is 5000-year-old traditional system of medicine based on the idea of balance in bodily systems and uses diet, herbal treatment, and yogic breathing. It can be traced back to India and is the oldest continuous natural and holistic medical system on the planet. Let me tell you, it is an incredible system that allows you to understand how unique you are, slow the aging process, live in balance with nature and much, much, more.

Ayurveda in Sanskrit is broken down into Ayus, which means life and Veda which means science of knowledge. Put it together and you have the science or knowledge of life. It comes from the core concept that we are all interconnected with nature.

There are five elements of the Universe within each of us: ether, air, fire, water, and earth. Now what if I told you that the three main energies that exist in nature also exist in us? Yes! The Tridosha System is made up of three energies: That is vata, which is air, ether; pitta which is fire, and kapha which is water and earth. Just like the MBTI quiz, you can take an Ayurvedic test to determine what dosha is the strongest within you. Your dosha can determine what time of the day is best for you to be productive, what kinds of foods you should eat, what time you should go to sleep, and more. You can book a Chaos Clarity call with me at www.jothidugar.com and we can dive deeper into an Ayurvedic test for you. That revelation lends itself to a really neat bodily awareness.

This awareness even goes as far as to tell you the signs and symptoms of a body out of balance. Each dosha has different bodily chaos responses. Those bodily chaos responses can present themselves as heartburn, diarrhea, acne, irritability, and more. Wouldn't you love to know what your bodily chaos responses are so you could prevent them before they happen? I hope you now see that we all have this authentic internal operating system. When it is aligned with nature, we are balanced and our operating system runs effortlessly. When out of whack, there are plenty of problems that need troubleshooting. But learning what potential problems can be is a great start to combating bad chaos.

# BAD CHAOS AND ENERGY

I'll be honest, chaos busters, this one could take up an entire book in and of itself. Your energy type and spatial energy affect you from the clothes you wear to your hairstyle, makeup, and even the colors around you. A painting on your wall can project a certain energy and contribute to the bad chaos in your life, without you ever meaning to invite that madness in your life to begin with. Woah, Jothi. Is there a test for this too?

Yes, friends. There is. Carol Tuttle teaches energy profiling. You can take her free quiz at www.caroltuttle.com. If you take this quiz, you will know not just the colors that you should wear but also your hairstyle, the type of makeup, the heaviness of the clothes that you wear. All of that plays a huge part on your own energy. When we're looking into energy management these are the ways you can set yourself up for success.

Remember when I discovered my energy type called for me to wear brighter and bolder colors in my work environment? The colors I was wearing (those blacks and greys) were not a match for my energy type. When I began to wear the bolder colors, I felt more like myself! Now I will say that if you are wearing the "wrong" color, that doesn't mean you'll be filled with negative energy. It simply means you will be blocking positive energy and prevent alignment with the universe.

As you may have guessed, you can cause a lot of bad chaos in your energy when you're blissfully unaware of your energy type. In fact, you're suppressing your energy. You're holding it hostage. You can't be buoyant and free if you're hiding behind greyscale heavy clothes. Energy tests are a lot of fun. When you ask someone "what do you think contributes to the chaos in your life?" Most people will respond with "stress." But this tricky bad chaos also contributes to the chaos. Everything around you can contribute to the chaos in your life. It is up to you to learn how to harmonize your mind, body, and energy to quiet that chaos and live your best life.

## CHAPTER 7 TOOLKIT

- Rip tide chaos is bad chaos, which is chaos that we are not keenly aware of.
- There are many tools and tests you can dive into to learn more about your personality types (MBTI), body type (Ayurveda), and energy type (Energy Profiling)
- Colors, hairstyles, your job, and the food you eat can all impact your bad chaos.

*Chapter 8*

# HARNESS THE POWER OF SURFER CHAOS (GOOD CHAOS)

**Pay attention to the things that make you feel alive –
then harness the power of that energy every moment
you can.**
-Jothi Dugar

Alright folks, we're finally here to the good chaos. Yes, this is the chaos we *want*, but you already knew that, right? That surfer chaos (good chaos) allows us to feel like a surfer riding those waves. We feel confident in ourselves and excited to be propelled forward into that blissful state that I know you are craving. Now, please don't panic if you haven't completely released your tsunami or rip tide chaos just yet.

You are not failing. I repeat. *You are not failing.*

This is completely normal.

Remember how many years you were inviting all of the chaos, the good, the bad, the ugly, into your life? Releasing the not so good chaos is going to take time. But guess what? You're aware of it. You have an arsenal of tools at your disposal from this book. With newfound confidence and excitement. Let's ride these surfer waves!

Jothi, what do you think is the single most thing that prevents people from inviting surfer chaos into their lives? Well, friends, there are a lot of factors. But I'd say, people are afraid of any chaos. The word chaos breeds anxiety in some. There is also this fear of the unknown and our obsessive desire to control every outcome imaginable. If something (like a delicious surfer wave) appears to be "too big," our insecurities and imposter syndrome will talk us out of riding that wave. Without the surfer chaos, though, our lives would be boring, right?

There would be no innovation or creativity. We'd never have the need to expand and grow. We'd just sit floating in our placid pond, never feeling excitement. If Alexander Graham Bell didn't ride the surfer chaos in his life, we might not have the telephone. If Mark Zuckerberg didn't push past doubt and fear and ride the surfer wave of Facebook, what would social networking look like today?

Surfer chaos is *amazing chaos.* By now, if I were to quiz you on the mind-body-energy connection, I have no doubt you would ace my test. We know that chaos starts in the mind. Whether that chaos is ugly or bad. Well, of course, good chaos starts in the mind too. And it is our very minds that can knock us off our surfboards and send us floating back to the refuge of the safe and peaceful shore.

Humans crave control. We analyze possible outcomes to events in an effort to prepare ourselves for the resolution. We plan, we prepare, we do everything to minimize risk. It might be something embedded in our DNA after years of evolution. You know, some animals got really cool fangs and humans got an intense complex and need to control everything around them to feel safe. In safety there is comfort. In comfort there is stagnancy.

When was the last time you were excited about something? Was it a big presentation? A cruise? A dinner party with friends? Excitement feels good. Excitement can override fear. That is exactly what you need to do to harness the power of the surfer chaos. When you start to get nervous, when the panic button gets pushed, you have to keep going.

It is a lot like the ocean, actually. If you're paddling out with your surfboard, you're going to have to get past the area where the waves break by the beach. If you're not careful, you could get knocked off your board before you make it to the deep water where the big waves are. Are you going to turn around?

No, you will keep paddling. By now, you've learned how to trust your intuition. We've done those exercises in previous chapters. By now you should know when things feel right. Your intuition is your trusty guide.

Do you know why? I'm serious! Do you know why your intuition is your guide? Well, it is because the universe points you in certain directions and uses your intuition to help you read those signs. The universe can make you so uncomfortable you have no choice but to move and try something different and that ends up being the path you were meant for all along. The universe puts certain people in your path because they are meant to play a role, either big or small, in your life. The universe has your back. Trust it.

Sometimes you feel opportunities coming and you know they are the right thing to do. Maybe you are a little nervous, but you know deep down in your heart this is what you want. You have to push past your fear. Yet there are other times, my friends, when you can't see that tremendous surfer wave ahead. You may be in the middle of tsunami chaos. However, if you remember that surfer chaos state of mind and visualize that feeling of excitement, it will carry you through the tsunami chaos.

Now, let's talk about visualization `Another way to capitalize on the exhilarating rush that surfer waves provide is to picture yourself riding them before you even get on your surfboard. I can't stress how important visualization is to your own personal success. You need to visualize your desired outcome before it happens. Believe it into existence. Visualization is incredibly powerful. Because the fact is your mind can't always distinguish what is real and what is imagined. Therefore, the more you manifest success in your mind, the more you will manifest success in your life. If you keep focusing on your present place you won't get where you want to be.

Remember, everything in life occurs twice, first in your mind, and second in your physical reality. Now, when I talk about visualization, it's using your whole body and making it an experiential session. Use all five senses to visualize your dreams as if it were happening now. Bring in that same energy into the present moment, and feel those high frequency positive vibrations now as if you already have what you want.

For example, let's say you want a loving, deep, connection with your partner. You want someone who has your back no matter what, is caring, and supportive. You do not necessarily have to visualize your current partner. The visualization doesn't always have to be that literal. You could instead, visualize yourself in a happy moment with your family or recall memories where you once felt the feeling you want to manifest once more. Pay attention to the things that make you feel alive. Find more of those things.

The happier, more fulfilled, more excited you are to live each day, the more you will radiate that positive vibration out to others. People love being around positive people. Positive vibrations are contagious in the best way. By surrounding yourself with others that have high vibrational energy, everyone wins.

Finally, and this is particularly important my friends. I want you to know that we are never really alone. We are always connected to other humans, to the environment, and to the energy around us. Even when you feel alone, try your best to give to others. But in the same vein, remember it is okay to take from time to time. When someone offers you help, you may want to decline for fear of inconveniencing them. My advice to you is, don't. When you decline help, you are depriving others of feeling fulfilled! That's not fair, is it?

Now, chaos busters, I have imparted all the wisdom I have on you. I hope you take each lesson to heart. I hope you now have a full understanding of ugly chaos, bad chaos, and tsunami chaos. I hope feel inspired to live your best life yet, to harness the power of chaos within you, and to build upon your self-awareness daily. Thank you for taking this journey with me.

## CHAPTER 8 TOOLKIT

- Surfer chaos is the good, exhilarating chaos that makes you feel alive
- You must push past your fear to reach those surfer waves
- Use your intuition as your guide
- Visualization is a powerful tool that can help you achieve a state of surfer chaos in the moment when you need it most.

Printed in the United States
By Bookmasters